TO:

....

FROM:

....

WHEN GRIEF *goes* DEEP

WHERE HEALING BEGINS

WHEN
GRIEF
goes
DEEP

WHERE HEALING BEGINS

Edited by

TIMOTHY J. BEALS

ZONDERVAN®

Library of Congress Cataloging-in-Publication Data

Title: When grief goes deep : where healing begins.
Description: Grand Rapids : Zondervan, [2023] | Summary: "The collection of devotions and prayers warmly offer inspiration and hope based in God's Word and his promises to those who have experienced loss. Each devotion includes a Scripture verse and prayer for healing"-- Provided by publisher.
Identifiers: LCCN 2022061122 | ISBN 9780310158059 (paperback) | ISBN 9780310158066 (epub)
Subjects: LCSH: Grief--Religious aspects--Christianity--Prayers and devotions. | Grief--Religious aspects--Christianity--Biblical teaching. | Healing--Religious aspects.--Christianity--Prayers and devotions. | Healing--Religious aspects--Christianity--Biblical teaching.
Classification: LCC BF575.G7 W474 2023 | DDC 155.9/37--dc23/eng/20230707
LC record available at https://lccn.loc.gov/2022061122

INTRODUCTION

D o you ever feel like many of the people in your life don't
understand the unique challenges you face as someone
walking through grief? Your loss has shifted the way you look
at and experience almost everything—sleeping, walking, eat-
ing, relationships. The way you order your priorities and your
routine.

Grief has changed everything about your life. At least it
may feel that way today. A dozen things can trigger grief every
hour—things that can be invisible to other people. We may feel
misunderstood because others often don't see our struggles and
don't "get it."

God does. More than anyone who has walked the face of
this earth, he understands grief. He also has something to say to
you about what you're going through. God knows your heart. He
knows your grief. He sees you and cares more deeply than you
could ever understand.

Each devotional in this collection is written by someone who
has been confronted by the challenges of grief. These readings are
not meant to be read certain days of the week or even in order.

Each reading is anchored to a relevant passage of Scripture, a key verse, and a closing prayer. I encourage you to begin each day's reading by first reflecting on God's Word. Then read through the devotion before praying and asking God how the Scripture passage applies to your life. The prayer is a starting point for a time of conversation with God—the One who knows and the One who cares.

Timothy J. Beals

1

Losing a Mate Is Losing a Part of Yourself

Read: Genesis 2:18–25

The first words of humankind in the Bible are poetic—Adam's ecstatic waking utterance capturing his joy in beholding a glorious new creation from his own body. "Bone of my bones and flesh of my flesh . . ." Then God crowns his handiwork by creating a marriage—joining man and woman into one flesh. And each wedding kiss creates this moment anew.

These words also carry with them the painful reality that losing a mate is losing part of yourself. Losing bone and flesh creates painful wounds and scars—wounds that need tending.

I'll never forget the words of the surgeon who said, "I'm so sorry, Mr. Beach. But your wife did not survive this procedure." His words took about three seconds to say. But their impact will affect me the rest of my life. Sue and I had been married eight years when she died at Mayo Clinic due to complications from the bone-marrow transplant process and prior treatments of chemotherapy and radiation. Five days before her death, we celebrated our eighth anniversary in her room in the Critical Care Unit.

Losing my wife began a process of change with many corollary losses: having children together and raising a family; building a log home; enjoying grandchildren; having a sense of identity as her husband, friend, and lover; having her as a best friend, confidant, and cheerleader; growing old together and sharing a legacy. These large losses pained me. Smaller ones pained me too: purple irises, Charley's Crab restaurant, her brownies.

In all of these losses, a part of me is lost. These losses are permanent in my heart and soul, and the scars remain tender.

When I read this beautiful poetry now, I also hear a tone of tragedy. I am happily remarried to a beautiful woman—another wedding kiss, another joining together as one flesh. But this new joining together as one does not undo the rending asunder of my first marriage.

What are the corollary losses in your life? Where do you feel most keenly the wound in yourself—in your own flesh and bone? Where do you most want God's love to enfold you and help you? Ask him now.

> *Dear Jesus, you have been waiting to be joined with your bride. You know this pain of separation. In the wideness of your mercy, help me to grieve well the loss of my spouse, part of my own flesh and bone. Amen.*

—————————— DAVE BEACH ——————————

2

God Sees Us and Does Not Abandon Us

Read: Genesis 16

When I was fifteen, my granddad was hospitalized. When I went to visit him, he was screaming, and my mom wouldn't let me go into his room. I sat in the hall and listened as he cried out in desperation. I heard every word.

"Jesus, dear Jesus. I want to come home. Jesus, please release me from this body. I want to come home, dear Jesus."

I listened to those words echo down the hall over and over. I now realize that my granddad had the same desire as Paul "to depart and be with Christ, which is better by far" (Philippians 1:23). Grandpa had been paralyzed and had suffered for years. He was a man of faith who believed God was with him.

I am reminded of Hagar, who fled from Sarai into the desert. My granddad must have felt as if he had been left in the desert. When Hagar was in the desert, the angel of the Lord told her, "Go back to your mistress and submit to her" (Genesis 16:9). The angel promised Hagar that her descendants would be "too numerous to count" (Genesis 16:10). After Hagar's encounter with the angel, she said, "You are the God who sees me" (Genesis 16:13).

When we are grieving, we may feel like we are in the desert. Yet it is when we are there that we can see God clearly. Hagar realized that while she was in the desert. She said, "I have now seen the One who sees me" (Genesis 16:13). In our grief, we can more clearly see God because he meets us in the desert to provide guidance and comfort.

God does not abandon us. While our family and friends may abandon us, God stays with us every step of the way. In John 14:18, Jesus promised, "I will not leave you as orphans; I will come to you." Although we may not feel like God is with us, we have to remember that "faith is confidence in what we hope for and assurance about what we do not see" (Hebrews 11:1).

When we are grieving and our hearts are crying out for comfort, God is there. He understands what we are experiencing. God comforts us (see 2 Corinthians 1:2–4). When we turn to God and pour out our hearts in grief, God reaches out and provides comfort to us—even when our friends and family cannot understand our heartache. Prayer provides an avenue for us to open our hearts to God.

God sees you. He's listening. Even when you can't find the words, he hears you.

> *God, I feel so alone. I don't know how I can cope. Please comfort me and help me know that you see me and love me. Amen.*

BETH ROBINSON

3

Choosing to Mourn

Read: Genesis 23

Abraham had been married to Sarah for a long time, and Scripture tells us he mourned deeply when she died. He didn't hide his tears or cry privately, and he sought to honor her with a proper burial. No one was left wondering how he felt about her death. Life would never be the same again for him, and he allowed his grief to "go public." He would need to learn to live without her because the option of living in a pre-loss world was over. His grief would either transform him or destroy him, but it wouldn't leave him the same.

Abraham didn't always have the freedom to choose the roles he would play in life, but he could choose how to play the roles he was given. Circumstances wouldn't make or break him. The same hot water that hardens an egg softens a carrot. He always had choices about how he would respond.

The loved one we grieve now was given to us as a gift, not a right. We can choose to thank God for the joy he or she brought. We can choose to vacate the premises of the past by asking, "What kind of person do I want to become as I progress through this grief?" Practice doesn't make perfect; it makes permanent, and we will continue to do what we have done in the past until we choose to learn another way. When we let go of something—or someone—we make room for something new. The pledge to never forget can become the pledge to never recover, but it's possible to give up the pain without giving up the precious memories.

Some of us are independent people who have always been givers, but now we need to receive. Giving is much easier than receiving. Choose to break ties one at a time. Clean out belongings when you are ready. Don't let others' discomfort be your guide. Only you can decide what you can handle. Choose what's important. Grief is not a bucket with a hole shot out of the bottom for all future joy to drain out. Your capacity for joy is far broader than you may realize now, and you can trust that God has sustained your life for a good purpose. Choose to cooperate with God in becoming all he has in mind for you.

> *Good Father, help me to focus on you and your promise to be with me in all that is ahead. I know the important thing is not where I'm standing but the direction in which I'm moving. When I feel I can't make it, help me to remember that because of you, I have everything I need for the days ahead. I choose you, God, and the growth that will transform my life as a result of this grief. Amen.*

DORIS SANFORD

Facing Your Emotions

Read: Genesis 37

When Jacob learned of his beloved son Joseph's (supposed) death, he did five striking things in response to his grief: he tore his clothes; he put on sackcloth; he mourned many days; he wept; he refused to be comforted. Our tendency might be to dismiss some of his reactions as culturally different, unusual. These reactions to grief, however, were common in ancient Near Eastern cultures. After observing our culture, I wonder if we might learn something from Jacob about facing grief.

We have intriguing expressions in American culture about showing grief and other strong emotions. They include "falling apart," "losing it," and "breaking down." We also assign emotions to either positive or negative categories. We place grief in the latter. Our language constructs our perception of grief and our preference for turning from grief rather than facing it.

I remember visitation at the funeral home following the death of my younger brother, Dick. When my friend John C. came through the line, he hugged me and I wept. Later, someone who had observed my reaction described it as "Dave lost it." After hearing this, I didn't want to make others feel uncomfortable, so I chose to hide my grief. I got the cultural message and let it shape my response to my grief. What messages have others given you about grief? How did they affect you?

In Dr. James Pennebaker's book *Opening Up: The Healing Power of Expressing Emotion*,[1] he cites several studies which indicate that we gain protection against harmful internal stress when we express emotions. We also gain the long-term benefits of decreased risks of future diseases and increased health in our immune system.

Jacob not only faced his grief but also embraced it. He put on sackcloth—a culturally accepted way of expressing grief—which was typically coarse black cloth made of goat's hair, much like wearing black in some cultures today. He wept and he mourned; he became a person who was acquainted with the pain of grief.

Jesus is also "a man of suffering, and familiar with pain" (Isaiah 53:3)—or as the King James Version puts it, "a man of sorrows, and acquainted with grief." He wept when his friend Lazarus died. God wants to develop the heart of Jesus, a man of sorrows, in us. What if not facing and embracing our grief means we are resisting this development? What if expressing grief is actually "coming together" rather than "falling apart"— our heart and spirit coming together with our body?

Dear Jesus, I choose to trust you. Form your heart in mine. Amen.

DAVE BEACH

5

God's Identity: I Am

Read: Exodus 3:1–17

In the conversation between Moses and God in Exodus 3, God refers to himself as I AM. Whenever God talks about his identity, we need to pay attention because his words affect how we move forward in our circumstances.

The name I AM speaks of God's relationship with his people, his character, his ability, his self-existence. And the term is present tense, that's who he is right now. He was I AM yesterday, he is I AM today, and he will be I AM—the name by which he's to be remembered from generation to generation.

In this Scripture passage in Exodus, God makes a few noteworthy comments when talking about his people in Egypt: (1) "I've seen their misery," (2) "I've heard them crying," (3) "I'm concerned about their suffering," (4) "I've come to rescue them." The people of Israel needed a reminder that God hadn't forgotten them and that he was big enough to handle their problems. We need that reminder, too, because we can easily forget truth when we are immersed in our sorrow. We live in a different time today, but God is the same. He sees our misery. He hears us crying. He's concerned about our suffering. And he will rescue us.

God's name expresses powerful messages.

- I am here for you always.
- I am able.
- I am accessible.
- I am faithful.
- I am your comforter.
- I am the giver of joy, peace, hope, and rest.
- I am love.
- I am everything you need.

If we think about who he is and really believe that what he says is true, our fears will dissipate.

In Isaiah 41:10, God says, "So do not fear, for I am with you; do not be dismayed, for I am your God. I will strengthen you and help you; I will uphold you with my righteous right hand."

Here's another way to think of it: So do not fear, for I AM is with you; do not be dismayed, for I AM is your God. I AM will strengthen you and help you; I AM will uphold you with his righteous right hand.

Our God is a God of presence. He's a God of promise. His name is I AM, and he says, "I will." We can take comfort in that.

God, because you are I AM, I don't need to worry or fear. I can rest in knowing that you're who you say you are and you'll be true to your word. Amen.

————————— TWILA BELK —————————

6

Letting Go

Read: Exodus 9:13–35

I can't let go." Ann's whispers were barely audible as she clutched at her chest while waves of intense pain washed over her. "Everyone else has moved on, but I just can't let go."

Three years after her son's unexpected death, Ann's grief was still fresh and raw. "I'm tormented every day," she cried. "What really happened? Was this God's plan, or did evil prevail? I just want my son back." Ann was agonizing over the unknowns of her terrible loss, looking for answers to comfort her.

Many of us are haunted by gnawing, unanswered questions following the death of our loved ones, especially when the surrounding circumstances are tragic or even mysterious. Amid our bewilderment and grief, we plead to understand God's redeeming purpose. "Where's your glory in this plan, Lord?" we ask.

When doubts bombard us, it's important that we don't rely on our own human reasoning but instead hold fast to God's Word. "Trust in the Lord with all your heart and lean not on your own understanding," Proverbs 3:5 says. Still, letting go with trust and acceptance is difficult.

Perhaps when everyone else appears to be going on with life, you're stuck, still clinging to what was and what could have been, unable to let go and surrender your expectations and dreams. Your faith wavers because life—even more, death—doesn't make sense. If so, you're not alone.

Moses had a few questions for God. As we see in today's reading, the Lord said to Moses, "Get up early in the morning, confront Pharaoh and say to him, 'This is what the LORD, the God of the Hebrews, says: Let my people go, so that they may worship me'" (Exodus 9:13). But earlier Moses had questioned God's plan. He pleaded with God to do things another way: "Who am I that I should go to Pharaoh and bring the Israelites out of Egypt?" (Exodus 3:11). "Pardon your servant, Lord. I have never been eloquent, neither in the past nor since you have spoken to your servant" (Exodus 4:10). "Pardon your servant, Lord. Please send someone else" (Exodus 4:13).

Riddled with tormenting doubts and fears, Moses eventually let go of his will and yielded his life to God's purpose.

It grieves God's heart when we, his people, are held captive, gripped by oppression. When we clutch our pain, we become enslaved as chains of bondage wrap around our soul. Conversely, peace comes when we surrender to God's will.

> *Faithful God, I open my hands and release all that I hold into your everlasting arms. Uphold me with your strong embrace as I let go and reach for the future. Amen.*

———— DAWN SCOTT DAMON ————

Time Does Not Heal

Read: Exodus 15:22–27

Time doesn't heal; it merely passes. Nothing about the passage of time automatically brings healing. The passage of time can bring bitterness, withdrawal, or guilt as well as growth. The loss of someone we love can be the purest pain we ever experience, and time is a friend and companion as we adjust to this new reality.

Grief takes time. Giving ourselves time to grieve is a good and necessary thing. Exodus 15:26 shows us that healing after a major loss is the result of action, not passive waiting. We have to forget about shortcuts because there aren't any.

Some of us did amazingly well at our loved one's funeral, and everyone applauded how well we handled our loss. But, of course, we were still operating under the "anesthesia" of numbness. The reality of life without our loved one wasn't really on our radar yet, so we functioned in a fog during the early weeks of grief. We looked better than we actually were. Shock protected us from going crazy. When the fog lifted, we found we had hard work to do to move through the pain, and it would take far longer than we ever expected. The crowd cleared and went back to their own lives, and we felt the emptiness of building a life without our loved one.

The work of grieving includes slowing down to feel, to listen to our loved one's favorite music, to take a quiet walk. It means taking time to cry, to hold our child's blanket, to ask for what we need. For some people, support groups are helpful, and for others talking to a close friend who can listen without interrupting is better. We need to be patient with ourselves whenever we "fall apart" when we'd rather be glued together.

The word *closure* is frequently linked to grief. It implies a belief that certain events allow us to put a lid on our loss and emotionally move on. But as attractive as that prospect is, there's no real closure to a major loss. Grief doesn't suddenly stop. It fades. We won't forget, and we don't want to forget. We will always remember even though our overwhelming feelings of grief lessen with time. Recovery doesn't imply we go back to being the person we used to be, but we do make peace with the loss. It takes time and hard work.

Have you made peace with your loss?

Father, I need your help for the slow, stuttering process of healing. I receive you as the one who has promised to never leave me to work it out alone. I choose to trust you today. Amen.

———————— DORIS SANFORD ————————

God Hears You When Life Isn't Fair

Read: Numbers 11:1–20

When I'm facing difficulty I didn't expect or anticipate, an idea sometimes knocks on the door of my faith. It whispers, "Life in Christ should be a gentle road. You shouldn't have to face this. It's not right." But when I view the panoramic canvas of God's deeds, I can't reconcile this whisper with today's Scripture text. When I look closer, I find that this idea may not be God's heart for me at all.

When we're suffering and squeezed between doubt and despair, the voice that says, "I don't deserve this" isn't our friend. Oh, the voice is right. It's not fair. Life shouldn't be this way. God didn't create the world this way, but the world we live in doesn't operate as God intended it to anymore. Nevertheless, when the world crushes us with its blows, God doesn't leave us alone. He first comes personally to hear and comfort, and then, through others, he provides the human touch and support we need.

In today's reading, Moses came to the edge of his ability and the end of his patience with the complaints of the Israelites.

When his people complained about the manna, he complained to God. Moses seemed to say, "Why is this so hard? Why me? I didn't ask for this job. I can't take it anymore."

God was concerned about Moses' pain, and he acted on the people's complaints. God responded by answering their request for meat and appointing new help for Moses. God allows us to come to the end of ourselves so we can learn real dependence. When we come to the end of our own energies, we can learn how to draw from the deep places of God's heart for us. Even the dark times have a purpose.

Decades ago, Charles Spurgeon wrote,

> It is because He loves us so much that He tries us by delaying his answers of peace. . . . Love closes the hand of divine bounty and restrains the outflow of favor when it sees that a solid gain will ensue from a period of trial. . . . It would be unwise to shorten such golden hours. The time of the promise corresponds with the time most enriching to the heart and soul.[2]

Has God delayed his answers? Does life seem unfair? Know that God's enrichment will flow from this time of grief in the days ahead.

> God, help me see when I am overloaded. I don't need to prove something to you through my effort. You promise to respond when I call on your name, regardless of my circumstances. Today, I just need your help. Amen.

———— TIMOTHY BURNS ————

9

Unanswered Questions

Read: Deuteronomy 29:22–29

Life is full of unanswered questions. These questions are exaggerated when we have suffered a major loss, especially when the loss is sudden or unexpected. When I lost my nineteen-year-old-daughter, Shannon, to suicide in 1991, my mind was full of questions: Why did she take her own life? What was so painful for her that death seemed better than life? Why didn't I see this coming?

And my most difficult questions were directed to God: If you are so good, why did you allow this to happen? Why didn't you let me know she was so depressed? You knew, God, before time began, that this was going to happen. Why her? Why us? Why me? Why did you give me this child only to take her away?

These and other questions ran through my mind over and over like a broken record. As I wandered through my grief journey over the weeks and months, I came to realize that life couldn't offer any definite answers. Thankfully, I gradually came to a place in my healing where the "why" questions became less important and the focus became "Where do I go from here?"

Linda Flatt, who lost her son to suicide, wrote, "The only

person (except for God) with the answers to my questions is unavailable to hear them. And it occurs to me that he might not know the answers himself."

Do we demonstrate a lack of faith when we ask questions such as these? I don't believe so. God understands our humanness. We want answers, want to figure things out, want to reach some level of understanding when difficult things happen to us. It is a natural human inclination to ask questions.

We may not, however, get the answers we seek. God has chosen to let us in on some of his secrets and to keep other things from us. "The secret things belong to the Lord our God" (Deuteronomy 29:29). His ways are not ours, and his thoughts are not ours (see Isaiah 55:8–9). There are reasons for what happens that we can't understand because of our limitations. Our finite minds simply can't understand the mind of God and his universe. We have to trust that he knows and that he has a plan for our lives. Through his Word and Holy Spirit, he has revealed to us what we need to know to follow, trust, and obey him.

God understands your pain, what you are going through, and the questions you may be asking. Take a few minutes to write out your questions, ask God for wisdom, and trust him with the answers.

Father, I come to you wanting to understand my loss and grief. I have questions but no answers. Help me to trust that you understand even when I don't. Amen.

SUE FOSTER

10

Anger Toward the One We Lost

Read: Deuteronomy 31:1–8

Before my father died, I had never mourned. I had moaned, bemoaned, and complained, but I had never truly mourned anything.

After my father's death, the overwhelming emotion I felt was anger. I was so mad at him for ignoring his health and for not taking care of himself. I was angry that he seemed to have lost his first love for Christ and been worn down by the cares of this world. I was disappointed that he hadn't taught me how to die with faith, in peace and full of hope.

I was angry we had wasted so much time. My heart ached that my opportunity to be a daughter to him was over and my kids wouldn't have a grandfather. There was nothing in me I could summon to even try to make it okay. I was utterly bereft, empty of everything except grief and rage.

Matthew 5:4 tells us, "Blessed are those who mourn, for they will be comforted." Anger doesn't sound like a spiritually appropriate response to death, but too often we make up what mourning is and what it should look like. Mourning is a deep and arduous task. When we mourn, we acknowledge that something is dead—a gift, a time, or a person—and we express our emotions about the fact rather than fighting the fact itself. Mourning isn't simply feeling sad until the sadness goes away.

It's common to feel angry when someone dies, but Christians can feel pressure to conform our mourning to what we think is more acceptable. The truth is, there are missed opportunities and disappointments even in the best relationships. In other relationships there can be abuse and neglect. Pretending to not be angry about things that went wrong or wrong things that were done to us won't make the feelings go away. It just breeds bitterness.

God is always with his people. We can lay claim to his promise to Joshua through Moses: "The Lord himself goes before you and will be with you; he will never leave you nor forsake you" (Deuteronomy 31:8). Mourning invites God into our loss. As the memories and emotions come upon us, it's as simple as talking to God about them. We don't have to filter anything. It's okay if our prayers are jagged. God isn't going anywhere. When we stand in the truth of our pain and wait for him, power is unleashed and healing begins.

God, thank you for promising to never leave me. I'm so glad I don't have to pretend with you. Please guide me through all my emotions and help me to give them all to you. I don't want to be bitter, but I don't know how to let go of this anger. Help me to feel your presence. Amen.

—————— ALISON HODGSON ——————

11

Past Losses Impact Today's Grief

Read: Deuteronomy 32:1–12

Our reactions to losses form patterns. We may deny, avoid, detach, rescue, and so on. Reactions modeled for us by our parents and stories they tell us also create patterns. These patterns are often quite persistent and enduring. They become a family legacy.

In today's reading, Moses told the Israelites to remember their family history—the lives and the deaths of prior generations. He reminded them how past relationships determined national and international boundaries (see Deuteronomy 32:7–9).

"You're too young to attend your mother's funeral," the father said to his six-year-old son and ten-year-old daughter. They stayed with a neighbor during the funeral and interment. The next day, the father removed from the house anything connected to the children's mother and burned her things. Later, when the father remarried, he told his children they were not to talk of their mother.

My friend Mike shared this story with me fifty years after his mother's death while he was struggling to cope with the death of his son. Some months after Mike's son died, waves of grief overwhelmed him. Mike was usually stoic and was considered a strong person, and his sudden and unpredictable tears were distressing. He was afraid of having a breakdown. He also could not understand why he was so angry with his wife for what he called her "obsession" with re-creating their son's life in pictures.

I asked Mike if he noticed similarities between how he moved through his mother's death and his response to his son's death. He first said, "No. That was so long ago. How could it?" However, he started to see similarities. He began to see ways in which his behavior resembled his father's—something of which he was not proud. He asked if I thought he could change.

This Scripture passage in Deuteronomy highlights how older generations shape the future of their families—particularly in the telling of family stories. As mature Christ-followers, we shouldn't underestimate the influence we have on our families just by responding to life as it happens. Becoming aware of reaction patterns and then examining them in light of God's Word and love requires an intentional choice. Let us choose to leave a legacy of responding well to loss.

Heavenly Father, you who are love, grant me wisdom to leave a legacy of faith and loving-kindness for my family and my friends. Help me to respond to loss in a way that nurtures hope and health in me and in others. Amen.

DAVE BEACH

Cling to God

Read: Deuteronomy 33:26–29

Losing a spiritual mentor can be paralyzing. It can feel as if the light has gone out and the world has gone black. You relied on your spiritual mentor for counsel, for direction, and for wisdom, and without them you don't know what to do.

The Israelites faced such a situation. They had followed Moses for forty years. He was their leader and their voice to God. He had turned the Nile into blood, separated the Red Sea, communed face-to-face with God, and given Israel the Law. In front of the Israelites was the river Jordan, and beyond that river was a land filled with giants and other obstacles.

As the people of Israel waited to enter the promised land, God called Moses up on Mount Nebo. But Moses never returned (see Deuteronomy 34). Surely the Israelites wondered how they would ever be able to carry out God's plans without Moses.

Before Moses died, he spoke a blessing over the twelve tribes of Israel (see Deuteronomy 33:1). After pronouncing a blessing over each tribe, he said, "The eternal God is your refuge, and underneath are the everlasting arms" (Deuteronomy 33:27). It was as if Moses was saying, "I am not your refuge. I am not the arm upon which you are to lean. I did not rescue you from Egypt. I did nothing but cling to God. So, Israel, cling to God! For he is your eternal refuge, and his arms are everlasting."

Without a spiritual guide, the road ahead is terrifying. But when spiritual leaders are taken from us, God asks that we put our faith in him, for it can be tempting to lean on the spirituality of others. We find our true source of strength in God. Jesus reveals God's plan for the "stranded" believer this way: "But very truly I tell you, it is for your good that I am going away. Unless I go away, the Advocate will not come to you; but if I go, I will send him to you. . . . But when he, the Spirit of truth, comes, he will guide you into all the truth" (John 16:7, 13).

Spiritual leaders are master "clingers." They are wise, they are loving, they are good because they follow God. Moses reminded Israel that when the great unknown knocks, the eternal God is not just nearby or next to or close, but he is protecting his children above, behind, and below.

God goes before the Christian into the unknown, into the land of giants. The grieving soul is not abandoned, is not alone. We must put our faith in God, trusting that beneath our frail spirit are the eternal God's everlasting arms.

Father, my spiritual leader is gone. I'm afraid of what's ahead, and I feel so alone without my mentor. Give me the faith to lean on you and trust in your everlasting arms. Amen.

DANIEL BERNSTROM

Where Do I Go from Here?

Read: Joshua 1:1–9

Moses was dead. The man who stretched out his hand—and by whom the Lord sent devastating plagues on the mighty Egyptian empire—no longer cast his long shadow over the Israelite camp. Into this void, God was calling someone else to accept Moses' mantle, and Joshua wasn't sure about his call.

Joshua had spent more time with Moses than any other person had. When Moses ascended Mount Sinai to receive the Ten Commandments, Joshua waited partway up the mountain for his friend's return. Joshua often walked with Moses when he left the camp to talk with God at the tent of meeting and had always been the first to see Moses emerge from the tent with his face shining with God's radiant glory. But now Moses was gone, and thousands of families looked to Joshua for their inspiration.

The rush of Joshua's heartbeat pounded in his ears. For the first time he understood what the weight of leadership had meant to his mentor and friend. He wondered if he was up for the job and if he could go on without his friend—even though he had been so confident years ago when he and Caleb had tried to convince the people to trust God and take the land.

God met Joshua in the place of his greatest need, and he will meet you there too. When we are convinced we can be successful on our own, God may meet us with silence. But we often hear him speak to us in our hours of despair and doubt because we are ready to listen. In those moments, he reminds us that our future is based on his promises and instruction.

- I will never leave you nor forsake you.
- Be strong and courageous.
- Be careful to obey me.
- Meditate on my Word.
- Do not be afraid or discouraged.
- I will be with you wherever you go.

God asked Joshua to look beyond his own energy and his fears, because God's promises were the basis of everything that would happen for the rest of Joshua's life.

Father God, When I am at the end of myself, remind me that you led me here and that your hand is ready to strongly support me. My responsibility is to learn, know, and believe the promises of your Word. You are the source of everything good. Amen.

—————— TIMOTHY BURNS ——————

14

Handled with Care

Read: Joshua 4

G od created us with the ability to remember. He uses memories of loved ones as part of our healing process. Our memories can be a sweet source of comfort after a loss. But if they are to comfort rather than cause pain, memories must be handled with care. The task can be difficult, particularly after the death of a child.

A friend of mine lost a child in a car accident shortly after Christmas many years ago. The next November I asked about her holiday plans. "We're going to my sister's in Phoenix," she said. "We want to be with family. But we're not ready to spend Christmas in our house without our daughter." They negotiated the anniversary of their daughter's death close to Christmas by creating distance from the previous year's memories. The distance made celebrating the holiday manageable for them and their two living children.

Deciding what to do with a child's possessions also requires careful handling and should not be done too quickly or left too long. For the sake of your living children, consider not making the child's room a shrine. Instead, as parents and siblings, select keepsakes for your individual grief journeys. Honor any last wishes your child had by distributing items according to your child's directives. Then, as a family, agree on what to do with remaining items. Donate them to charity, perhaps, or to families who will make good use of them.

Tiffany handled her pain without creating a shrine for her son, Ethan, when he died a week after his birth. She keeps some of his clothes in a box because she can't bear to part with them. "I miss what won't be," she said. "Sometimes I open the box of clothes to smell him. It's hard to be without him, but if I immerse myself in his things, I don't miss him as much."

God created us to remember the people we love after they die. When Jesus introduced communion during the Last Supper, he said, "Do this in remembrance of me" (Luke 22:19). Similarly, memories and mementos of those we love, handled carefully, allow us to remember our time on earth together with joy and gratitude. "Do this," God whispers into broken, hurting hearts, "in remembrance of those you love."

Lord, I'm thankful for my memories and mementos of my beloved. Please heal my heart until every remembrance becomes joy, comfort, and assurance of your hand at work in my life. Amen.

JOLENE PHILO

15

A Familiar Path Home

Read: Joshua 24:1–28

I turned onto the familiar road, and the dark clouds finally dumped their rain. Like a flood down a narrow canyon, water fell in waves, not drops. In this blinding torrent, even the familiar turned treacherous. I was driving home, trying to find my comfort, my safe haven, but I couldn't see the road. So I began looking for familiar landmarks instead of watching the road. I turned the corner under a favorite coffee shop's bright yellow sign and passed the well-lit gas station on the left. The landmarks told me that in a few more blocks, I could drive into my garage, dry and safe from the deluge.

As the garage door closed behind me, I sat in my car and shook. The road home is easy when life is bright and clear. Yet today I needed every fragment of the familiar to help me find my way.

Your grief may have hit you like an unwanted deluge, and with it waves of blinding emotion—fear, sorrow, guilt, and loss—have come crashing into your life. The emotional torrents can obscure your view. Suddenly everyday tasks are all but impossible. A good friend said that after his wife died, some days he wondered if he would make it the next twelve minutes, much less the next twelve hours, before he would crawl back into bed and pull the blanket over his head.

As Joshua's life moved toward the end, he looked back at the personal history he, Moses, and God had written for the people of Israel. Since their escape from Egypt, God had proven he was faithful, involved, connected, attentive, and personally committed to Israel. The Israelites no longer thought of the Lord as Moses' God. He was their God, their Protector, Savior, Shepherd, and Friend. Joshua, as one of his last duties as their leader, advised them to stay connected to their ever-present Protector and Guide, even when Joshua was no longer with them.

We don't get to pick when grief hits as a blinding torrent. We can, however, follow the markers that will guide us safely home. As the prophet Jeremiah wrote, "Set up road signs; put up guideposts. Take note of the highway, the road that you take" (Jeremiah 31:21).

When we walk daily with God in the good times, we are more ready for the trials and better equipped to survive the storms. What are the guideposts that will guide you through the storms of your grief?

> *God, today I'm grieving, but I remember talking and walking with you when the skies were clear. Help me remember those days. Even though the storms of life rage today, I know I can find the path into your sheltering arms. Amen.*

———— TIMOTHY BURNS ————

When Grief Strikes

Read: Judges 7:1–25

Grief strikes at the most unexpected times. One minute you're smiling and thinking, *I'm moving ahead. I really am.* The next minute something triggers a memory and rips away the thin scab covering your wounded soul. You gasp in pain. Tears course down your cheeks. Grief camps out in your aching heart again, and you can't move forward.

Gideon, one of the judges God raised up to deliver the Israelites from their oppressors, was naturally feeling anxious after the Lord instructed him to pare down his army to only three hundred men. Realizing that Gideon's faith was wavering in light of the vast enemy forces arrayed against him, God advised him, "If you are afraid to attack, go down to the camp with your servant Purah and listen to what they are saying. Afterward, you will be encouraged to attack the camp" (Judges 7:10–11). God's instructions worked. Accompanied by his servant Purah, who was probably also his armor-bearer, Gideon received all the encouragement he needed to rout the enemy.

When grief attacks, God wants us to reach out for a friend and move forward. Naomi calls one such friend a "gift" from

God. She and DeAnn were friends for fourteen years before their babies were born. A few years later, their sons both died of the same kind of cancer. "We went through it together and grieved together and knew exactly how the other felt at all times," Naomi said. "We are able to go through our cycles of grief together. We understand how the other thinks, so we have each other always, under any circumstances. And that's an incredible gift."

Our God knows you need a friend to help you process your grief. In Romans 8:32 the apostle Paul recorded this promise: "He who did not spare his own Son, but gave him up for us all—how will he not also, along with him, graciously give us all things?"

God promises to provide all we need when grief strikes. So ask God, the God who knows the agony of watching a child die, for someone to walk beside you when you can't move forward alone. As surely as he brought Purah to Gideon and DeAnn to Naomi, he will bring you a friend too.

> *God, you gave Gideon a friend when he was threatened by a vast enemy army. I need a friend like that when grief overwhelms my heart. You know how much I need someone to talk to about this devastating loss. I trust you to provide the right friend at the right time. Amen.*

JOLENE PHILO

He Won't Turn Away, Even If You Do

Read: Judges 10:6–16

Are you like me? When things are going well, it's easy for me to forget to make time for God. After all, I've got so much good stuff going on that I don't have time for prayer. Of course, sooner or later something bad happens, and without hesitation I take my broken heart to God, expecting him to drop everything and respond to me.

And here's the amazing thing: he does. God's response reminds me of the way he responded to the Israelites in Judges 10:16 after they'd forsaken him: "Then they got rid of the foreign gods among them and served the Lord. And he could bear Israel's misery no longer."

After the way they had betrayed God, serving other gods despite his consistent faithfulness to them, it would have been reasonable for the Israelites to expect God to turn away from them when they were in need. But the merciful God we serve didn't turn away. And he won't turn away from you either.

Perhaps, like me, you've been guilty of ignoring God when

things were going your way. Perhaps you've even turned your back on God and walked away from him for a long period of time, and you feel as if he would never be willing to take you back.

And now you're facing this painful loss. The pain is unbearable, and you don't think you can make it alone. Judges 10:16 promises that you don't have to if you turn to God.

Perhaps you've admitted to yourself that you've not been as faithful to God as you should have been. Admit it to him, as the Israelites did in Judges 10:15. He doesn't want you to bear this hurt alone. If you earnestly ask for his help in this difficult season, he will not ignore your plea. God is grieving with you.

It's easy to feel as if God stands ready to help other people but not us, that somehow our less-than-perfect relationship with him makes us unacceptable in his sight. But the truth is this: Jesus reconciled his children to himself on the cross, and nothing can separate us from the love of God.

Self-imposed separation from God may have kept you from reaching out to him in the past. Take the first step to tear down that wall today. The Sustainer and Redeemer of all creation stands waiting to embrace you with his calming, healing presence and to comfort you and give you deep, abiding peace.

Your first step is as easy as three words: "Help me, Father."

God, help me to not be afraid to admit my need for you in this season of grief. Thank you that you forgive me and do not hold my past sins against me. Amen.

STEVE SILER

18

Moving Forward

Read: Ruth 1

As I boarded the plane for Rhode Island at the tender age of eighteen, I knew my life would never be the same. That leap of faith led to four years of rigorous studies and leadership training as a midshipman at the United States Naval Academy. When I tossed my cover (hat) in the air with 964 of my classmates, I again left a family of friends, mentors, and loved ones. I went on to serve six years of active service as an officer in the United States Marine Corps. I spent eleven years training and serving America with a fearless group of people who became family. I loved serving, and I grieved when I had to let the military go, but it was only in letting go of the old that God opened the door for new opportunities.

Ruth's life was also filled with grief at the loss of family. I am sure she grieved when her husband died. And she must have grieved that no children had been born into the union, leaving her with no sons to secure her livelihood. As a young, childless widow, she was left with little hope in life. She faced two choices: return to her biological family or go into uncharted waters with her mother-in-law, Naomi.

We all face crucial choices in life. Like me, you may need to leave a promising situation because God has something different in mind, or, like Ruth, you may be tempted to remain in what appears to be a comfortable situation though it may not be good for you. At every crossroads in life, we must remember the words of God, "I have set before you life and death, blessings and curses. Now choose life, so that you and your children may live" (Deuteronomy 30:19). The choice to say that God's people are your people and their God is your God (see Ruth 1:16) is a choice to sacrificially move forward, no matter the cost. Moving forward with God is choosing life.

Lord, you determined the times set for me and the places where I would live. You adopted me into a new family, and therefore I will never be alone. Thank you for rewarding me with life. Amen.

—— NATASHA SISTRUNK ROBINSON ——

19

The Comforting Power
of Friendship

Read: Ruth 2

R uth was a sojourner in a foreign land. Because of her love and friendship with her mother-in-law, Naomi, Ruth left her homeland after the death of her husband to follow Naomi to Judah. There she met Boaz, a relative of Naomi's, while she was gathering grain in his field. Boaz befriended Ruth, allowed her to take all the grain she needed, and granted her favor with himself and his servants.

Ruth left all she knew—her country, family, and friends—to follow Naomi because she loved her. This had to be a great loss for her. If you have ever moved to a place where you knew no one, you can understand how difficult this was for Ruth. What helped Ruth adjust to her new home was the love and friendship of Naomi and the new friendship of Boaz.

You're grieving. You've had a loss and probably feel like you are a sojourner in a foreign land. As you navigate your journey, you need a friend or friends to travel with you. Naomi was grieving the loss of her husband and her two sons and the potential loss of her daughters-in-law. How comforting and encouraging it must have been for her to have Ruth want to go with her to Judah. God gives us a model for friendship in the relationship between Naomi and Ruth. Because of the common bond between them, they were able to encourage and comfort each other at the time of their greatest need.

Who is a Ruth or Naomi in your life? Do you have someone who will "stick like glue" to you as you grieve your loss? Perhaps this is a person who has had a loss similar to yours and who understands better than anyone else some of what you are going through. You now have a common bond, and a friendship can be formed or strengthened, even if only for the season of your grieving.

Don't be afraid to reach out to others in your time of need. Allow others to comfort and encourage you. People want to help. This is not the time for you to "go it alone."

God gave us relationships not only for the good times but also to be a comfort in the most difficult times. Ecclesiastes 4:12 tells us, "Though one may be overpowered, two can defend themselves. A cord of three strands is not quickly broken." There is power and strength in friendship.

> *Jesus, you are a friend to me. Help me to allow others into my life at this time to show me your love and comfort as I journey into this foreign land of grief. Amen.*

SUE FOSTER

20

Life After the Death of a Spouse

Read: Ruth 3–4

The book of Ruth might well be renamed the story of Naomi, as the story begins and ends with her. To appreciate the ending, we need to understand her story. The beginning of the book of Ruth describes several losses. First, Naomi loses her home as her husband takes her and their sons away from Bethlehem to Moab. Then her husband dies, leaving her alone with her two sons. They marry Moabite women, but then her sons die, leaving Naomi alone with their wives. As she prepares to return to her home in Bethlehem, her daughter-in-law Orpah decides to stay in Moab. Only Ruth, her other daughter-in-law, remains with her as she travels home to Judah. The theme of the beginning of Naomi's story is overwhelming: "leaving and being left."

The death of our spouse is a "leaving and being left" part of our story too. Standing in the cemetery and seeing for the first time the cold gravestone with my wife's name etched on it, I felt alone and empty—left behind.

Naomi keenly felt her grief. Arriving home in Bethlehem, she said to her friends, "Don't call me Naomi. . . . [Naomi means "pleasant"] Call me Mara [Mara means "bitter"], because the

Almighty has made my life very bitter. I went away full, but the Lord has brought me back empty. Why call me Naomi? The Lord has afflicted me; the Almighty has brought misfortune upon me" (Ruth 1:20–21). Naomi the pleasant became Mara the bitter.

Alone and without provision or a home of their own, Naomi and Ruth needed to trust someone—a guardian-redeemer—for provision and safety. Often, when we're in a vulnerable place, trusting is the hardest thing to do, isn't it? I think God placed this story in the Bible especially for people like you and me who've lost a spouse, been left behind, known the affliction of grief and need to trust someone for provision.

The man they trust, Boaz, proves faithful, not only by providing for Ruth but also by marrying her. Boaz redeems by purchasing the land of Naomi; he renews and restores Naomi's family by having a son with Ruth.

The Lord *did not leave* Naomi without a redeemer; he renewed her life. May this be your comfort today: The Lord has not left you without a redeemer; he will renew your life.

> *Jesus, great redeemer, my loneliness and the feeling of having been left behind often overwhelm me. The future is hard to imagine. Waves of grief seem unending. In faith, I choose to place my uncertain future in your heart and hands. Renew my life and sustain me in your grace, redeemer of souls. Amen.*

DAVE BEACH

21

The God of Comfort

Read: 1 Samuel 1

I was pregnant with my first child, and the kicking and rolling I could feel in my belly surprised me.

"God is amazing," I thought. "Who could orchestrate a miracle like this?"

My husband and I were having a son, and we named him Elijah after the prophet and my maternal grandfather. We wanted our son's name to be great and for him to follow the Lord. I was five months pregnant the weekend I purchased my baby's first outfits and teddy bear. The following day, I was rushed to the emergency room, and he was gone.

In my grief, I cried out to God and meditated on the words of Hannah: "I prayed for this child, and the Lord has granted me what I asked of him. So now I give him to the Lord. For his whole life he will be given over to the Lord" (1 Samuel 1:27–28).

To say that it is difficult to let go of a child is a massive understatement. In Ecclesiastes, the Teacher states, "There is a time for everything, and a season for every activity under the heavens: a time to be born and a time to die, a time to plant and a time to uproot, a time to kill and a time to heal, a time to tear down and a time to build, a time to weep and a time to laugh, a time to mourn and a time to dance" (Ecclesiastes 3:1–4).

Knowing that death is a normal part of life does not make facing it easier, though releasing a child does help us understand, on a micro scale, the magnitude of God's grace and love for us in his willingness to give up his own Son. "For God so loved the world that he gave his one and only Son" (John 3:16). God's love and grace are far-reaching, and this is good news. In the midst of our sorrow, God the Father, who released his only Son, understands our burdens and hears and answers our prayers. He will not leave us comfortless. "Praise be to the God and Father of our Lord Jesus Christ, the Father of compassion and the God of all comfort, who comforts us in all our troubles, so that we can comfort those in any trouble with the comfort we ourselves receive from God. For just as we share abundantly in the sufferings of Christ, so also our comfort abounds through Christ" (2 Corinthians 1:3–5).

> *Lord, I thank you that you are the God of grace and time. Thank you that I will see my child again. Thank you for so freely giving your son on my behalf. I continue to hope in you. Amen.*

─────── NATASHA SISTRUNK ROBINSON ───────

What God Looks For

Read: 1 Samuel 16:1–13

Samuel had a job to do, and he had some preconceived notions about how to do it. Therefore, when he arrived in Bethlehem, he was surprised by what he found. After Samuel asked Jesse and his boys to go through a cleansing ritual (see 1 Samuel 16:5), the prophet began to inspect Jesse's sons with one thing in mind: pick out a winner.

He had come to anoint one of Jesse's eight sons as the next king of Israel—to replace the disappointing initial monarch, Saul. Samuel, though directed by God in his search, was impressed by human characteristics God wasn't looking for. He was looking in the wrong place for the future king.

We sometimes get a little confused at what we are looking at. Have you checked the labels on your grocery items lately? You may be getting less than you thought you were getting. According to an article in *U.S. News & World Report*,[3] some manufacturers are selling us the same size packages we are accustomed to but they are putting less of the product in the box. For example, a box of well-known detergent that once held 61 ounces now contains only 55. Same size box, less soap.

How something is wrapped doesn't show us what's inside. That's true with people as well. We can wrap ourselves in the same packaging every day—nice clothes, friendly smile—yet still be less than what we appear to be. That's where Samuel comes into the picture. And that's where grief also comes in.

The story of Samuel's search for a king to replace Saul shows that God looks deeper than outward appearances. The prophet Samuel was interested in packaging; God was interested in contents. The first of Jesse's sons who paraded in front of Samuel in this Old Testament *X Factor* TV-show-type event was the farmer's firstborn, Eliab. Samuel took one look and said, "Surely the Lord's anointed stands here before the Lord" (1 Samuel 16:6).

But he was wrong. Samuel had yet to learn this all-important truth: "People look at the outward appearance, but the Lord looks at the heart" (1 Samuel 16:7). And the heart God was looking for belonged to a kid named David. He may not have been as strapping and handsome as Eliab, but David had the right contents.

God is looking beyond our "packaging" to the grief we carry. He sees beneath the surface and cares about our hearts. He's not fooled by the outward display we sometimes put on for others.

In God's eyes, it's the contents and our hearts that count!

> *Creator God, you see us as no one else does. You see our heartache and grief. Thank you for understanding us better than anyone else ever could. Amen.*

——————— DAVE BRANON ———————

23

Express Emotions Freely

Read: 2 Samuel 1

In today's reading, we encounter traumatic wartime deaths. David received word that many fellow soldiers of Israel were killed during a battle with the Amalekites. The dead included King Saul and Saul's son Jonathan—David's best friend.

David and his men tore their clothes, mourned, wept, and fasted the rest of the day. When we remember that they were at war against a bitter enemy, we find their response more impressive and, perhaps, informative.

The first thing they do is suspend the daily activities of life as warriors and freely express emotion. Their reactions are not common for modern warriors, but they honored in a noble way the strong bonds of soldier brothers. As Medal of Honor recipient US Army captain Jack Jacobs said during an MSNBC interview, "When times are really difficult, we fight to preserve the union and accomplish the mission. But most of all, we fight for each other. If you ask anyone who has fought, anywhere ever, for this country, he'll tell you the same thing: We fight for each other."[4] This strong bond intensifies grief.

Freely expressing this powerful emotion not only honors the

dead but also honors the power of deep grief. One of the difficulties in post-traumatic stress is fear of these emotions. Many combat veterans struggling with post-traumatic stress do not fear the memories of events; rather, they fear their intense emotional response to them. In our reading today, warriors respond by freely expressing their grief.

David not only openly laments those killed in action but also composes a communal lament and makes it a part of standard operating procedure. He orders soldiers and civilians alike to mourn with him. "I grieve for you, Jonathan my brother; you were very dear to me" (2 Samuel 1:26). There is healing power in communal lament, which counters the isolation we feel when left to mourn privately.

Families of grieving soldiers feel it too. Hundreds of thousands of families regularly deal with the private emotions of family members who are veterans of war. As a nation, we need a better way to honor these wounds of war. Perhaps this story from long ago can be helpful. Are you a veteran carrying private, unexpressed grief from the fog of war? Are you a family member struggling to understand a loved one's behavior? Perhaps this story of individual, communal, and national lament can help us see the value of giving voice to our suffering and expressing emotions freely.

Father God, help me find ways to freely express, like David, my emotions. Amen.

DAVID BEACH

24

Treasures in the Valley of Grief

Read: 2 Samuel 9

W hen my mom was diagnosed with terminal brain cancer, all I could see was the horror of losing her. Out of pain and desperation, I pleaded with the Lord to save her. My mom, on the other hand, immediately put her life in God's hands. She led the way for me to trust a loving and almighty God, no matter the outcome.

God showered countless blessings and miracles on my family during the 108 days my mom lived after her diagnosis. Even as our hearts were breaking, we shared unprecedented love, unending forgiveness, and pure joy. I could never have imagined when she was diagnosed the gifts God had in store for us; they were treasures in the valley of grief. Without the mercy of God, we would have been left devastated and empty-handed. But to this day, because of God's goodness, the miracles continue.

In 2 Samuel 9, we read about Mephibosheth, Jonathan's disabled son, who fell from his nurse's arms when he was five as they were fleeing to safety and, for the rest of his life, was "lame in both feet" (2 Samuel 4:4). To honor his friend Jonathan, King David showed mercy to Mephibosheth, restoring his family's land to him and inviting him to dine at the king's table for the rest of his life. Because Mephibosheth had the king's mercy, favor, and protection, he was able to live in peace and prosperity.

Like Mephibosheth, we too are the recipients of grace. We don't deserve God's grace, but he doesn't rule according to human standards; he rules by love and grace. Because of the gift of redemption given by his own Son, God invites us to dine at his table as his beloved children.

The world, apart from Jesus, looks at our loss and says, "Poor you." It tells us we're doomed to live with empty hands and broken hearts. But God says our sorrow never has to be the end of the story. He promises that when we love and trust him, he'll comfort and heal us—he can even use our pain for good. Out of his mercy, God has chosen to adopt us as his children and give us all the unfathomable riches and gifts associated with our royal position.

When we choose to trust Jesus, even in the midst of our greatest pain and loss, miracles happen. Our eyes open to a world of grace and joy we never could have imagined. The world can't make sense of our joy in the middle of our grief. It's a gift from a loving and almighty King who always keeps his promises.

> *Dear Jesus, my heart is broken. As I grieve, I look to you for comfort. Please help me trust you completely. Thank you for the good you have in store for me. I pray you will strengthen my faith as I open my heart to you.*

LORI LARA

25

God's Promises Don't Fail

Read: 1 Kings 8:54–61

Joel 2:25 states, "I will repay you for the years the locusts have eaten." God gave me this promise concerning my stolen childhood. Among the losses I grieved was a broken, dysfunctional relationship with my father. God spoke to my heart months before my father's cancer diagnosis, telling me he would restore my relationship with my dad. But in those final months of his life, that seemed impossible.

I watched as cancer eroded his body. My tall, strong father came to resemble a prisoner of war. I hadn't spent any meaningful time with him in over twenty-five years, and here I was, along with my sisters, sitting by his bedside day after day, caring for him. But over the next few months, my dad and I talked about everything. We cried, we laughed, we sang the hymns of my childhood faith, and he shared deeply from his heart.

Then one day he tenderly took my hand and told me he loved me and would miss me. I squeezed my daddy's fragile hand—the same hand that had stolen my innocence. In one glorious moment, I knew God's promise had been fulfilled. He'd restored the relationship the enemy had stolen.

Has God given you promises? Seemingly impossible promises? Keep believing and don't ever give up. "The Lord is trustworthy in all he promises and faithful in all he does. The Lord upholds all who fall and lifts up all who are bowed down" (Psalm 145:13–14).

In life's dark moments, we're tempted to doubt the promises God gave us in the light. It's not uncommon to feel as though the hopes we held deep in our heart died with the loss of a loved one. But Numbers 23:19 reveals God's character. "God is not human, that he should lie, not a human being, that he should change his mind. . . . Does he promise and not fulfill?"

When dark times assail us, we must remind ourselves what's true about God:

- He is good, even when I hurt.
- He is faithful, even when I'm not.
- He is wise, even when I'm lost and confused.

When we cling to the unchanging truth of God's Word—especially in times of grief—and declare his promises to be true, we'll find the dark clouds that blind us dissolving into the light of God's glorious presence. Though we sorrow for a night, God's joy does indeed come with the morning.

> *Lord, I trust your unfailing love. I believe you keep your promises. I know you will not fail me. I will not doubt in the darkness what you've promised me in the light. Amen.*

—————— DAWN SCOTT DAMON ——————

26

Feeling Alone

Read: 1 Kings 19:9–18; Psalm 46:1–3

The day I became a grandmother was one of the happiest days of my life. It was also one of the most difficult. Watching my very loved daughter suffer was hard on me, even though I knew the end of the story would be wonderful. People were there to care, hover, and assist, but the work was her own. Our heavenly Father must feel the same way about those who grieve and feel alone in a painful "labor." He stands by—loving, encouraging, and, as the psalmist wrote, providing "refuge and strength" (Psalm 46:1). Our growth through grief is in some ways like childbirth, and the Great Physician knows the purpose of our story, which is maturity in Christ now and life forever with him in heaven.

Death ends a lifetime, but it does not end a relationship. The person is gone from our physical world but not gone from memory. Some who grieve have never lived alone. Every noise in the house at night is scary. In our early grief, Sundays are terrible days. Sitting alone at church and at dinner at home are painful reminders that life has changed. It takes a long time to not feel married. We see friends, but they don't mention our loved one's name, as if the one we loved never existed. Our grief feels invisible to others. How can the world continue on as if nothing has happened?

Most of us long for someone to come in and take over. We don't want to be asked what we need because we have no idea. One young mom said she felt like she needed a "keeper." If there is ever a time to plead temporary insanity, this is it.

In the middle of this awful aloneness, God offers to do for us what no human can ever do. When we sit in darkness, he will be our light. He is the one who can restore our souls, our energy, our hope, and our joy. He will meet us at every corner. He is there and will not fail us. We pray and cry. We pray and pace. We pray as we toss and turn. We are learning to trust his plan.

Our loved one's life was not "cut short." It was completed. And like Elijah, sometimes we are called to kiss goodbye the things we call dear as we press into God's call to move forward. Like Elijah, be reminded that our first priority—always—is to stop and stand in the presence of the Lord and listen for the comfort of his voice.

> *God, you will never leave me alone. I cling to you now. Fill this sense of aloneness with your loving presence. I know your goal in my life is not that I "get over" this grief but that I grow through it. I choose to trust you. Amen.*

DORIS SANFORD

27

What Do You Have in Your House?

Read: 2 Kings 4:1–7

The distraught widow approached Elisha. Her husband was dead, leaving behind a mountain of debt. Her sons could become slaves. Everyone knew her husband had been a God-fearing man. Together, they were supposed to live a long, prosperous, and blessed life. Now he was gone. We don't know her name, but we do know she was reeling in the loss, trying to figure out how to face tomorrow.

Obviously, she and her husband hadn't made any contingency plans, and she didn't have any job skills. The widow couldn't pick up a sickle and winnowing fork and head out to the fields to earn a living in her male-dominated culture. And the creditor was knocking on the door demanding payment or her sons. As she felt her life crumbling around her, she reached out to Elisha.

"What do you have in your house?" Elisha asked. He seemed to be asking, "What can you do with what you have? I want you to take your eyes off all the problems and focus on what you do have in your possession."

The widow might have replied, "What do you mean, what do I have in my house? Weren't you listening? My husband is gone. I have two young sons. They'll take them away if I don't pay what my husband owes. We have no food right now, let alone for next week. What do I have in my house? I came here because of what I don't have. I don't have my husband! I'm alone!" And after Elisha told her what to do with her olive oil, she might have said, "If you don't have any better ideas, I won't have my sons much longer either."

But the widow listened to Elisha, and through him God provided the miracle that solved her financial problems. But more important, Elisha's gentle question helped the widow take her eyes off the huge problem she faced and take control of what remained. He gave her the steps she could take so she could begin to close the door on the life that once was and step into the life that lay ahead.

Sometimes God calms the storm, and sometimes he calms us. In either case, God waits for us to look up and surrender the things we can't control. Then he helps us embrace what we can.

> *Father, I need you. I'm standing here with my arms full of everything I thought was important. Help me put them down one by one and turn my attention to what you would have me do and be. Amen.*

TIMOTHY BURNS

28

Gentle Whisper

Read: 2 Kings 19:9–19

As I lay in a hospital bed, I was told the horrific news that my husband, Doug, and I could lose our first child before her birth. Yet God was in charge, and on April 17, 1979, the Almighty blessed us with a healthy 7 pound, 13 ounce daughter.

But it wasn't long after our daughter's miracle birth that Doug and I were told she would be our only biological child. The news was devastating. For us, it was a deep loss. We had long dreamed of having several children grace our life and fill our home. The news of our loss was not expected; quite the contrary. We felt like someone or something had invaded our home and stolen a precious piece of our lives.

It wasn't long into our journey as a family that we would hear cruel comments—even from friends—such as, "You're not really a mother if you only have one child." What was I supposed to do with comments like that? Occasionally, our daughter would ask why she did not have siblings. The reality of our situation quietly cut into my heart like a knife. While we could not alter our circumstances, we believed God was still in charge and we would be comforted by his "gentle whisper" (1 Kings 19:12).

When we grieve, the "gentle whisper" of God's Spirit can stir in us. When I hear the voice of God, it's often a call to action, not a call to be tranquil or silent. There was nothing quiet inside me when God delivered the devastating news that we could lose our first child. Yet I had an overwhelming sense of God's gentle whisper telling me everything was going to be all right.

One of the psalmists in his turmoil wrote, "Today, if only you would hear his voice, 'Do not harden your hearts'" (Psalm 95:7–8).

While traveling in Israel, I was fascinated as I watched the shepherds with their sheep. The sheep knew their master's voice. The shepherds never seemed concerned if a little lamb began to wander away. When the shepherd spoke, the lamb listened and without hesitation went back where it belonged. King Hezekiah also displayed an obedience similar to one of those sheep. He listened to and did right by the Lord. He placed his faith in God's strength rather than his own when faced with what he felt were overwhelming circumstances (see 2 Kings 19:9–19).

Have you suffered loss? Listen for the Shepherd's promptings. Then respond with worship to his call to return to the safety of his arms, and you will find the strength to trust him as he speaks to you in the still, small moments.

> *Father, thank you for the still, small voice of your Holy Spirit. Thank you for Hezekiah as a model of worshiping and trusting in you. I want to worship just like that. Amen.*

DONNA FAGERSTROM

29

Devotion in Bad Times

Read: 2 Kings 20:1–11

Author and speaker Francis Chan tells the story of Dennis Guglielmetti, a successful Christian businessman working for a billion-dollar developer as vice president for learning and organization. He served at his church, handing out doughnuts to church members Sunday after Sunday. One Sunday in the fall of 2008, his pastor stopped by where Dennis was serving doughnuts and asked him how he was doing. Dennis, his speech slurred, confessed that something was wrong. By December of that year, Dennis was diagnosed with ALS (amyotrophic lateral sclerosis, or Lou Gehrig's disease), a disease that causes nerve and muscle cells to die. He was forced to retire from his job. He moved to Alabama and waited to die. At most, the doctors said, he had five years to live.

King Hezekiah was given similar news by the prophet Isaiah. Isaiah came to the sick king and said, "This is what the Lord says: Put your house in order, because you are going to die; you will not recover" (2 Kings 20:1). The news shocked Hezekiah, who was about thirty-seven years old at the time. He had been faithful, he had taken strong measures against idolatry, and he had kept the law of Moses (see 2 Kings 18:3–6). In despair, he turned his face to the wall and cried. "Remember, Lord," Hezekiah prayed, "how I have walked before you faithfully and with wholehearted devotion and have done what is good in your eyes" (2 Kings 20:3).

Dennis Guglielmetti, like Hezekiah, admitted to feeling sorry for himself and questioning God. He wondered, "Why me?" and "Why now?" Despite the horrible news, Dennis held fast to God. "Things happen in Jesus' perfect timing," he said.

Sometimes death comes slowly. How does one stay devoted to God in bad times?

1. Live out the remaining days, weeks, or years with a Christ-centered focus, leaning on him.
2. Seek to serve others and leave a legacy of service.
3. Treasure heaven. If your treasure is where your heart is, then "store up for yourselves treasures in heaven, where moths and vermin do not destroy, and where thieves do not break in and steal." (Matthew 6:20–21).

Remember that a life centered on God and service and focused on the glory of seeing Christ and his heaven provides us the strength to endure the moments of heartache and bitter weeping. For as the apostle Paul proclaimed, "For to me, to live is Christ and to die is gain" (Philippians 1:21).

Father, I don't know why you have allowed this to happen to me. Help me as I reach to you for strength. Amen.

———— DANIEL BERNSTROM ————

30

Run to God

Read: 1 Chronicles 14:8–17

For years I pushed away the truth that Mom was terminally ill. The thought made me want to run to the nearest doctor or mental health professional so we could find a way to make it all right. I wanted to deny that her final journey would be long and excruciating and that I would be able to do little about it.

I was forced to face the truth the day my self-sufficient father collapsed in my arms, crying for his wife. I knew in that moment I faced a choice: turn to my own limited resources or run into God's arms.

When David faced the threat of death at his enemy's hands, his first response was to ask God what to do. "Shall I go and attack the Philistines?" (1 Chronicles 14:10). David refused to make plans before he consulted God. He didn't rely on common sense. He didn't appeal to his closest friends or the best military advisers. He stopped in his tracks and asked God what to do.

When we face death and grief, common sense cries out for us to try to find a way out of the pain. David knew he was facing a battle. But he didn't turn to his own wisdom or the wisdom of counselors. He consulted God.

And David even asked God to assure him of a win. "Will you deliver them into my hands?" (verse 10). In other words, "Tell me your plan for me, and I'll trust you to be the sovereign God who saves his children."

When death threatens, it's easy to think it's our job to beat back the enemy. But our job is to turn to God and ask for direction, then to listen for his answers, knowing he secures deliverance for us and for our loved one—here and eternally.

David's source of confidence is revealed in 1 Chronicles 14:2: "David knew that *the LORD had established him as king over Israel and that his kingdom had been highly exalted for the sake of his people Israel*" (emphasis added). David knew his life's purpose was nestled in God's bigger plan for the nation of Israel and beyond.

When we see our life and our loved one's life as part of God's bigger plan, we can live with purpose in spite of our pain. We find the confidence to ask, "Shall I go . . . ?"

What are you facing today? Run to God and ask, "Shall I go?" Know that you, like David, can trust God to deal with the enemy you face today.

> *Father, before I take a step or make a decision, I come to you today and ask, "Shall I go?" Help me to trust you as you deliver my enemies into my hands. In Jesus' name I pray. Amen.*

SHELLY BEACH

31

God's Sustaining Grace

Read: 1 Chronicles 16:11

At a routine twenty-week ultrasound with our second child, we received news that no parent expects to hear. Our daughter Chloe was diagnosed in utero with a rare chromosomal abnormality, a condition that was incompatible with life. Our options included continuing the pregnancy to term—if she made it to term—or terminating the pregnancy. We entrusted Chloe's life and death into the care of our heavenly Father and continued the pregnancy as long as possible, knowing that she would die shortly after birth. Chloe was born at thirty-two weeks and lived for forty-five minutes, each minute spent cradled in our arms.

When we received news of the diagnosis, I was determined to cherish each day of those last twelve weeks I carried her. I knew, however, that each day also meant we were one day closer to saying goodbye. Still, God's sustaining grace met us in that place of challenge that required perseverance.

James 1:2–4 says, "Consider it pure joy, my brothers and sisters, whenever you face trials of many kinds, because you know that the testing of your faith produces perseverance. Let perseverance finish its work so that you may be mature and complete, not lacking anything." Embracing such instruction may seem absurd, especially if you are in the trenches of your grief. How can anyone "consider it pure joy" when they are in the midst of a trial? The key is to rejoice in the Savior, who walks with you through your trial.

Such perspective comes first from knowing and embracing the promise found in Romans 5:8: "But God demonstrates his own love for us in this: While we were still sinners, Christ died for us." This message of true biblical hope brings three elements of understanding to the pain of our suffering:

- Peace: Through faith in Christ, we can have peace with God. Peace with God is a prerequisite to experiencing the peace of God.
- Purpose: We may not understand why suffering occurs, but we can trust that the result of our suffering has meaning far greater than we could imagine.
- Perspective: When grounded in our faith, we begin to see life—even the most painful parts of life—with eyes fixed on eternity.

By God's sustaining grace, may you cling to the hope God has reserved for you.

Lord, thank you for making a way for me to have peace with you, through your Son, Jesus. Help me to trust in your sustaining grace. You are my hope. Amen.

TESKE DRAKE

32

With Your Whole Heart

Read: 1 Chronicles 28

Some of grief's storms find their way to our doors unexpectedly, like a summer snow or a thunderstorm at harvest time. But grief isn't always unexpected. Grief often is the distant figure we've watched for years walk up the road to our threshold. The family that says goodbye to their mom or dad after a long, full life suffers no less grief than a family that loses a young parent or child unexpectedly.

Toward the end of his life, Solomon, traditionally assumed to be the author of Ecclesiastes, wrote, "There is a time for everything, and a season for every activity under the heavens: a time to be born and a time to die, a time to plant and a time to uproot, a time to kill and a time to heal, a time to tear down and a time to build" (Ecclesiastes 3:1–3). Maybe his feelings grew from watching his father navigate both triumph and failure. David chose Solomon to take his place on the throne of Israel, and Solomon very likely got a closer look into his father's heart than his brothers did. As a result, he stepped into his father's large footprints with an uncommon confidence. He'd watched his father navigate political power struggles and military campaigns, and at the end of his life, David stood arm in arm with his son and with his God.

David's advice to his beloved son Solomon rested on the foundation of everyday decisions, not just a few big events. We remember David as the young lad who killed Goliath, the warrior who routed the Philistines, and the lustful adulterer who murdered Bathsheba's husband. Yet in between these milestones were years of quiet faithfulness. So as David made the proclamation over his son to the people in today's passage, the depth of his devotion was a well he'd dug daily, a few shovelfuls at a time. When he looked his son in the eye and reminded him to acknowledge the Lord wholeheartedly and willingly, David was pouring into his son's life a legacy that would never fade, even long after he was gone.

When we walk through grief and loss or any other sudden life change, the twists and turns are easier to navigate if we've regularly spent time with God. If life hasn't been a consistent walk or a surrendered pilgrimage for you, perhaps today God is calling you to begin a new journey with him.

Father, every day I have the option to surrender to you and trust you with everything I have. Your mercies are new every morning, and each dawn is a new opportunity to give you my whole heart. Draw me to you and teach me how to live with wholehearted devotion to you. Amen.

TIMOTHY BURNS

33

Take Courage from Others

Read: Ezra 10:1–17

John and Matt met in a divorce care ministry, both bent under the weight of broken relationships. As fathers, they were able to share their parenting experience, which opened the door to a lasting friendship. Together they sorted out single parenthood and navigated decisions on dating, relating to their kids, and rebuilding their finances. Matt explained:

> John was the one person that I knew could relate to how I felt. I talked to my pastor and my counselor. I prayed and stayed connected to my church, but those relationships got twisted as my identity evolved from head of a married family to single dad. However, I could always call John, and knew that he walked the same path. I let him see who I really was. I don't know how I would have healed without his friendship.

God made us in his image, and even he exists in a community of Father, Son, and Spirit. From the first pages of Genesis to the last page of Revelation, the Bible reveals God as our loving Creator, who says and demonstrates, "It's not good for a person to be alone" (see Genesis 2:18). We need people even when we don't want to. We love to share victories in a crowd of friends, but when we are lying on the ground unable to get up, Jesus' words—"Come to me, all you who are weary and burdened" (Matthew 11:28)—are most often fulfilled in the context of community.

The context of Ezra's story in today's reading is as complex as the questions faced after the sudden loss of a loved one or an unexpected divorce. Ezra led a contingent of Jews back to Jerusalem after well over a century of captivity in Babylon. He discovered that some of the men, including some priests and Levites, had violated their covenant with the Lord—perhaps in part because of a shortage of Jewish women—by marrying women from the neighboring pagan peoples. To restore their walk with God, the community of God's people faced life-changing decisions.

Alone, we sometimes make right decisions. When we're with a friend, we have a better chance of following through on what we say we believe when we're faced with a tough choice. But standing in a community, with a group of friends who know and love us, we find strength to face difficult decisions. In community, it doesn't matter if we're perfect, whole, tattered, or broken. We're no longer alone.

In your grief, seek out a like-hearted community of friends and receive the hope you need.

> Father God, I've learned the bad habit of trying to do life on my own. Lord, please lead me to a faith-filled community. Amen.

TIMOTHY BURNS

34

Positioning Ourselves in Prayer

Read: Nehemiah 1

When King Nebuchadnezzar of Babylon attacked Jerusalem in 586 BC, he battered and broke down the protective walls around it and destroyed the city and its temple. More than 140 years later, Nehemiah's great distress was not caused by Nebuchadnezzar's destruction but by the episode recorded in Ezra 4:7–23. The Jews had rebuilt the temple and started to rebuild the walls, but because of the protests of some neighboring officials, King Artaxerxes ordered them to stop.

Nehemiah was devastated to learn that the wall and the gates to the city were still in ruins. Scripture says he wept and mourned for days. His grieving actually could have been weeks or months. Nehemiah was inconsolable, and he turned to what he knew: he fasted and prayed for God's intervention.

Nehemiah was a man of considerable influence with direct access to King Artaxerxes—the man who had stopped the Jewish efforts at rebuilding Jerusalem's wall—but he recognized that the true source of help was from the God of heaven. Nehemiah might have been tempted to rely on his power, position, and influence with the king to change his people's situation, but he didn't.

Instead, he wanted God's best for the nation, so he called on the mighty power of God.

Grief has the ability to shrink our perspective to the size of the pain we are feeling, but Nehemiah didn't let that happen. Despite the personal anguish he felt, Nehemiah stayed connected to God's larger plan for his people. He immediately responded to the horrible news with prayer and positioned himself to participate in God's healing of the entire nation.

Did Nehemiah "set aside" his grief while he prayed and fasted? No. His grief became the fuel for his prayers. While he prayed, Nehemiah openly grieved before the Lord. He never denied his pain or pushed it away. Nehemiah allowed God to use his pain, and because he did he became a conduit of restoration.

When we are grieving, it's important to remember that we live within a larger context. Family, friends, coworkers, neighbors, and others have been affected by the same loss we are experiencing. They need our prayers and God's intervention just as we do. God hears our prayers. He heals our broken hearts.

Lord Jesus, don't let me live as a prisoner of my own distress, my own grief. May the pain I feel become my fuel for prayer to you, the living God. When all I see around is destruction, help me to position myself in prayer so I can be a conduit of healing to all those affected by this incredible loss. Amen.

———— DONNA TALLMAN ————

35

Wisdom and Grace in Grieving

Read: Nehemiah 2:1–8

No matter how good our intentions might be, grieving can become complicated. When my mother died, I gave clear instructions to funeral home personnel to remove the Bible our family had displayed in Mom's casket during her visitation. We would never have buried my mother with her beloved Bible, and a family member had requested to keep it as a treasured heirloom. But hours after her interment, I noticed that her Bible was not among the possessions the funeral home had returned to us.

Family members had deferred all major decisions regarding my mother's funeral to me, so I called the funeral home director, who apologized profusely for the oversight. He assured me the Bible could be "retrieved" and returned to the family the next day. The decision seemed reasonable to me. However, other family members saw the matter differently—and were unsettled at the idea. Our responses in the moments that followed required us to practice tact, wisdom, and grace.

The great Nehemiah also needed a solution to a problem. He mourned for days after receiving news that the Jewish people's attempts to rebuild the wall of Jerusalem, destroyed well over a century earlier, had been stopped by order of King Artaxerxes—the very ruler whom Nehemiah served (see Ezra 4:7–23). He was the cupbearer to the Persian king (see Nehemiah 1:11), which put him in an important position of trust. Nehemiah longed to rebuild Jerusalem, but he needed help from the king.

When King Artaxerxes noticed Nehemiah's sadness and asked about it, Nehemiah exercised diplomacy, tact, and wisdom. He didn't refer to Jerusalem by name, but called it "the city where my ancestors are buried" (Nehemiah 2:3; see also verse 5). He was hoping to stir the king's sympathy, and it worked. Nehemiah laid out a thoughtful plan, including an estimate of the amount of time he would be away, documents he would need for safe travel, and timber required for building. His carefully planned requests were all granted by the king.

In our grief, we are often tempted to let our emotions lead, and we sometimes act without forethought. But we are best served when we set aside our pain, develop a plan, and use grace, tact, diplomacy, and discretion in presenting it. We seldom grieve alone. We often must face the ruins of our past, relationships we once loved and might long to rebuild. And rebuilding means allowing our raw emotions to give way to the higher priorities of love and restoration and healing.

> *Father, please grant me the wisdom to know how to rebuild with wisdom, grace, and abundant love for others. Help me to learn to depend on you for all that I need. Amen.*

SHELLY BEACH

36

When Not to Run Away

Read: Nehemiah 6:1–13

Greg and Samantha had taken Jaxon into their home, and after three months they made plans to adopt him. But nine-year-old Jaxon refused to hug them or refer to them as his parents. Greg and Samantha were disappointed and grieving. Their dream of being parents wasn't what they had envisioned. They'd believed Jaxon would be grateful to be adopted and would be an enthusiastic member of their family.

Fortunately, Greg and Samantha were wise like Nehemiah. When one of his enemies recommended that Nehemiah take refuge inside the temple "because men are coming to kill you," he responded, "Should a man like me run away? Or should someone like me go into the temple to save his life? I will not go!" (Nehemiah 6:10–11). (As a layman, he was not permitted to enter the sanctuary.) Even if the threat against his life was real, Nehemiah was not a coward who would run into hiding. Nor would he violate the law to spare his life.

Greg and Samantha understood that they needed to hang in there and make a choice to love a child who wasn't ready to love them.

Perhaps grief has made you want to run. Loss can make it difficult to invest emotionally. Perhaps you have invested in a relationship—even at a price—and the investment hasn't been reciprocated. When you find yourself in this situation, you have to make choices of how to respond rather than letting emotions drive your behavior.

While you are grieving your loss, remember God may be preparing you for another dream. We plan our course, but God guides our steps (see Proverbs 16:9).

You can find great comfort in God's promise in Luke 6:38: "Give, and it will be given to you. A good measure, pressed down, shaken together and running over, will be poured into your lap. For with the measure you use, it will be measured to you." No matter how much you give, God will give more back to you than you can possibly give to others.

Grief makes it difficult for us to see beyond our pain, but the benefits of investing in relationships are long-term. God calls us to have courage. When the temptation comes to run, always head in the direction of truth and love. Where will that path take you today?

Father, provide me with the strength to hang in there when I want to run. Fill me with your Spirit so that I have the emotional energy to give to others even when I am grieving. Help me learn to love others the way you love me. Amen.

BETH ROBINSON

37

The Joy of the Lord Is Your Strength

Read: Nehemiah 8:1–12

H ow do you do it?" curious friends and acquaintances asked Maree as she recovered from a tragic accident that took the life of her mother. "You've gone through so much, yet you always seem so strong and calm."

People admired the way Maree responded. She had experienced many trials in her life, but she kept an upbeat attitude and sweet spirit. Her secret? The joy of the Lord. And because others noticed the evidence of her relationship with Christ, Maree had opportunities to share her faith with them.

During the celebration of the Festival of Trumpets, the crowd was weeping—rightly so—as they listened to Ezra the priest reading God's Word. But repentance must not become self-centered remorse, but instead should issue into joy in God's forgiving goodness. Nehemiah, the governor, told the people it was time for them to stop weeping and enjoy some good food and sweet drinks. "This day is holy to our Lord. Do not grieve, for the joy of the Lord is your strength" (Nehemiah 8:10).

But how is it possible to have joy when troubles surround us and our heart hurts? The key is found in what we focus on. If we dwell on our hardships, pain, and sorrows, they become overwhelming and sap our strength. If we concentrate on God's attributes and turn our thoughts to gratitude, a deep and unshakable peace will enter our heart and we will gain strength.

In *Choosing Gratitude: Your Journey to Joy*,[5] Nancy Leigh DeMoss writes, "Choosing gratitude means choosing joy. But that choice doesn't come without effort and intentionality. It's a choice that requires constantly renewing my mind with the truth of God's Word, setting my heart to savor God and His gifts, and disciplining my tongue to speak words that reflect His goodness and grace—until a grateful spirit becomes my reflexive response to all of life."

Recording a list of things you're grateful for is helpful for maintaining a positive outlook. Has someone extended kindness? Write it down. Did God provide for you in an amazing way? Write it down. Review your list periodically to keep remembering God's goodness.

Praise and gratitude keep you face-to-face with God. When you're face-to-face with him, you experience joy. Psalm 16:11 says, "You will fill me with joy in your presence." That's where you'll find strength.

> *Lord, joy and strength come from you. Help me keep my focus on your goodness. Amen.*

——————— TWILA BELK ———————

38

Anger in Grieving

Read: Job 2

P eople grieve differently, but we all share a common thread in grief: denial, anger, bargaining, depression, and finally acceptance . . . or not. Once shock and disbelief subside, the next stage of the grieving process emerges—anger:

- anger toward the one who died,
- anger toward yourself for not being able to prevent the loss, and
- anger toward God for allowing it.

Grieving is a God-given process that helps us transition from the loss of our old reality to the discovery of a new reality. The anger stage can be messy and frightening to watch or to express. But anger is an important, normal, healthy response to a significant loss. Like most emotions, anger can be either a positive or a negative force. Productive anger provides a passage to get through a loss. Toxic anger, however, clings, festers, and taints. Turned inward, toxic anger turns into depression.

Job was tempted and tested by Satan. He showed trust in his God and patience with his circumstances when he lost his wealth and lifestyle. Then Job and his wife lost all ten of their children. They must have been overwhelmed by emotion. Unfortunately, the misfortunes didn't end there: Job was struck with painful sores on his entire body.

Job's wife, whether out of hatred of God for what he had done to Job or out of a desire that her husband's misery should soon be ended, urged him to provoke God to administer the final stroke due to all who curse him. In her anger, she shouted at Job, "Are you still maintaining your integrity? Curse God and die!" (Job 2:9). And the anger expressed, in this instance, certainly wasn't healthy.

It may be hard for you to see anger as simply a part of the grieving process. This stage may be the most difficult for you to move beyond. Grieving is necessary, but it's meant to end. Good and sad memories will remain, but you will go on.

God never promises freedom from loss, disappointment, or pain. He does promise to be our strength and to bring something good from loss—if we allow him to. Grieving is meant to last for a time and bring us to acceptance and our new normal. So express your healthy anger—even toward God. He can take it. Let him bring you to the end of your grieving and to his promised peace.

In Jesus' name and through the power of the Holy Spirit, help me, Lord, to grieve well. Help me feel your loving arms around me, supporting and holding me in my mourning. Thank you for the hope I have in Christ. Amen.

SANDRA SCOTT

39

Living with Uncontrollable Emotions

Read: Job 6:1–13

Lorraine received a call from the police to come home immediately. A man had slipped in through an unlocked door while her sixteen-year-old daughter was alone. When his rape attempt failed, he stabbed her, killing her. Then he waited. When Lorraine's fourteen-year-old daughter arrived a few hours later, the man forced her to the basement, raped her, slit her wrists, stabbed her, and repeatedly slashed her throat. By a miracle, she survived.

"Grief shrouded me in total darkness," Lorraine said about the days that followed. "As time passed, anger took over. Depression engulfed me and led me to a frightening alley of suicidal thoughts. The voice of Satan followed me and filled me with angst and delusions."

The story of Job speaks about those same uncontrollable feelings. "If only my anguish could be weighed and all my misery be placed on the scales! It would surely outweigh the sand of the seas," Job cried (Job 6:2–3).

Satan uses these emotions to tempt us and pull us away from

God. Oswald Chambers says that "Satan does not tempt us to do wrong things; he tempts us in order to make us lose what God has put into us by regeneration . . . the possibility of being of value to God. He does not come on the line of tempting us to sin, but on the line of shifting the point of view, and only the Spirit of God can detect this as a temptation of the devil."[6]

When Satan uses uncontrollable emotions to rob us of the value we can have for God's kingdom, only God can walk us through that valley. Job knew neither his wife nor his friends could help him or give him the answers he wanted. He had to take his emotions and questions to the altar of the Almighty: "Teach me, and I will be quiet," Job pleaded (Job 6:24).

Pastor Jim Cymbala observes, "God does his most stunning work where things seem hopeless."[7]

Will you let him do "stunning work" in your heart? That's what he longs to do. If you can't control your emotions, it may be that you have not allowed them to flow unrestrained at his feet. Let them flow now, and don't hold anything back. He will embrace your pain, your fear, and any other emotion you feel. Cry out to him today, just like Job did.

> *Lord, I surrender my emotions to you and call on the Holy Spirit to pray the words I can't pray right now. Please give me the peace that is beyond all understanding. In Jesus' name I pray. Amen.*

— MARIA KECKLER —

40

Being Honest About Our Doubts

Read: Job 7:1–10

Mom's cancer diagnosis sent me tumbling. My mom? Pink-cheeked, skin-glowing Mom? Mom was seventy-eight, but she was aging well. She exercised multiple ways daily: swimming, walking, biking, and even weight lifting. For years she had cared well for herself. She even had been the first woman on our California block in the 1970s to jog. And now cancer? How could this be? She was too healthy to have cancer.

Two weeks before this cancer diagnosis, a doctor had attributed her sudden digestion problem to acid reflux. Couldn't we go back to that diagnosis? We couldn't. Instead my family and I had to face the bitter truth: Mom had stage 3 cancer. A few days later, doctors whisked her into surgery, where she underwent an extensive procedure that left her weak and altered. She was no longer who she had been. Her appetite, her strength, her independence—gone. Even her taste buds didn't want to function properly.

Her diagnosis forced me to observe something I didn't want

to see: My parents will die. I will die. Job names our vulnerability well: "Remember, O God, that my life is but a breath; my eyes will never see happiness again" (Job 7:7).

As I watch my mother's sudden and unfamiliar vulnerability, I'm unable to save her or restore her health. I cannot replace parts of her digestive tract that are no longer there. How I would if I could. Seeing her fragility angers me. Why doesn't God heal her? Why does he let this happen to us?

In chapter 7, verses 1–3, Job places his doubts and vulnerabilities before God. He doesn't talk himself out of them. Instead, Job entrusts them to God. He says, "Do not mortals have hard service on earth? Are not their days like those of hired laborers? Like a slave longing for the evening shadows, or a hired laborer waiting to be paid, so I have been allotted months of futility, and nights of misery have been assigned to me."

Job names the hardships we endure—our wearying seasons of sorrow. While naming them, though, he keeps his face turned toward God. He keeps this conversation of lament within his relationship to God. Through this he models how I, too, can confine and direct to God my sorrow, confusion, and doubt.

Lord, you know how vulnerable we are physically, mentally, emotionally, spiritually. You know everything, including my sorrows and doubts. Help me to recognize when I doubt you and to confide my doubt in you. You love me and wish to see me through the times that knot my faith. Amen.

CYNTHIA BEACH

41

Maintaining a Sense of Humor

Read: Job 8:20–22

When my friend Michael asked me to be a pallbearer at his father's funeral, I was honored. But I'm clumsy by nature, and in the days leading up to the service I found myself imagining the worst.

On the day of the service, Michael was also a pallbearer and called out directions as we carried the casket up the hill. The cemetery was in the Hollywood Hills of Southern California. Many famous celebrities have been laid to rest in this beautiful location overlooking the east San Fernando Valley. My friend has always had a wonderful sense of humor. Nevertheless, I was caught by surprise when we reached the top of the hill and Michael called out, "Turn left at Bette Davis!"

Maybe Michael sensed the anxiety of his friends or his comment was his way of dealing with his own tension. But from that moment, the ceremony became more relaxed, and we were just good friends helping a "brother" say goodbye to his dad.

Let's face it. Funerals aren't funny. Some people might even think humor is inappropriate at somber events like funerals. Yet as we reflect on the lives of those we've loved, it's inevitable that we'll recall times when our loved ones made us laugh or brought us joy by doing something fun or just plain silly.

Proverbs 14:13 tells us that "even in laughter the heart may ache." Mourning means remembering, and in the remembering the gentle grace of humor surfaces to lighten our moments and make the bitter bittersweet.

Days and weeks will inevitably pass when we feel as if we will never laugh again. During those days, the weight of sadness can feel as if it's too much to bear. When those days come—and they will—we can remember the ironic words Bildad spoke to Job: "Surely God does not reject one who is blameless or strengthen the hands of evildoers. He will yet fill your mouth with laughter and your lips with shouts of joy" (Job 8:20–21). Bildad would find out that he spoke more accurately than he realized, as "the Lord blessed the latter part of Job's life more than the former part" (Job 42:12). Job would get the last laugh!

If you don't feel like laughing today, don't be concerned. You needn't force your emotions or pretend. Grief takes time, and everyone works through it on their own timeline. As your heart heals, grief will become less like a smothering blanket and more like a panel in the quilt of your life.

The laughter will one day return.

Father, help me remember that you make room for laughter, even in the middle of tears. Help me believe that you give me permission to laugh even in grief. Amen.

STEVE SILER

42

God is Preparing Heroes

Read: Job 13:13–19

When the soldier arrived at Mary's door telling her that her son had died at an army base in Frieberg, Germany, her world crashed down. At first she was in shock and kept thinking that any day she would wake up and the nightmare would be over. But that was not to be, and she had a military burial to plan.

As time passed, Mary was filled with overwhelming anger. All she wanted to do was run away from God, but where would she go? She told God it hurt too much to even talk to him, much less pray. He had the power to protect her son. She had prayed daily for his protection and had trusted that God would take care of him. So why hadn't he? In the darkness of the valley of the shadow of death, she struggled and kept asking, "Why?"

Mary had to make a decision. All her years as a Christian told her not to give up on God . . . that he had a bigger plan. All she could do was echo Job's cry in Job 13:15, "Though he slay [my son], yet will I hope in him" (emphasis added). She made the decision to hope in God, repeating that verse over and over until once again she trusted him. It took a long time.

The story of Job can be hard to read when we go through

inexplicable loss. Through no fault of his own, Job endured pain and hardship. He never truly understood God's purpose for allowing his pain. Yet as we look back on his story and example, we see that God was preparing a hero—one who stands as an example of trusting God in the midst of unbearable pain and loss.

As believers, we find ourselves repeating the right Christian phrases. "All things work together for good" we offer when life doesn't go as we plan. But it isn't until we walk through the darkest hour that our faith is truly tested. At this point, our training begins, especially when we can't see any good in our loss or pain.

If you never understand "why," will you still trust him? Will you echo Job's words, "Though he slay me, yet will I hope in him"? Your pain may be too deep right now to answer that question. But you can begin repeating those words over and over again until they become ingrained in your heart and your mind. God may be preparing you to be a hero right now.

> *Lord, I can't understand why you have chosen to allow this loss in my life. Help me to endure the test and the training you have entrusted to me. I will choose to hope in you. Amen.*

MARIA KECKLER

43

The Essential Source of Comfort

Read: Job 16:1–5

During the early months of numbing disbelief over the loss of my husband, I basked in the comfort of friends. Sure, I heard an insensitive comment now and then from a "miserable comforter" or two, as Job experienced. For the most part, though, I was blessed with loving friends. It was enough.

Enough, that is, until the reality of my loss hit with its most searing pain, and I knew beyond the truth in my head into the depths of my heart that Bill wasn't coming back. The grass settling over his grave and the monument with the date of his death screamed the truth.

When we experience the first rawness of our grief, we have only one place to go to fill the empty chasm that yawns inside of us: straight into the waiting arms of God. After surviving imprisonment in a concentration camp, Corrie ten Boom based her ministry to others on this statement: "No matter how deep the pit, God's love is deeper still." This God of love reaches down into the deep places of our pain and sorrow to heal those things we find difficult to talk about and the most painful to acknowledge.

Job's three friends didn't help him at all in his grief. They would have been of more value to him if they had continued to sit in silence as they had for the first seven days and nights of their sympathy visit (see Job 2:13).

Instead, after Job spoke from his aching heart, they began to argue with him, criticize him, and accuse him of wrongdoing. God's response to this is in Job 42:7 as he speaks to Eliphaz the Temanite: "I am angry with you and your two friends, because you have not spoken the truth about me, as my servant Job has." In the end, after Job was found true to God in his grief, God comforted him and prospered him once again (see Job 42:10–17).

Like Job, we too long for comfort in our loss.

"The God of all comfort" (2 Corinthians 1:3) beckons us. Jesus encourages us, saying, "Come to me, all you who are weary and burdened, and I will give you rest. Take my yoke upon you and learn from me, for I am gentle and humble in heart, and you will find rest for your souls" (Matthew 11:28–29).

God's heart toward us is gentle. He doesn't add to our grief as the three friends did to Job after his massive losses. He offers us rest in the midst of our sorrow.

Only God can satisfy our soul with his loving comfort. Go to him with your heartache. He's waiting to take your sorrows.

Oh, God, only you can fill me up in the dark depths of my grief. In you I find rest and encouragement. You've become my all in all. Amen.

SANDI ELZINGA

44

Removing the Root of Bitterness

Read: Job 23:2

She lived with all of the hopes, dreams, and aspirations of any young woman, and soon her dreams were realized. She had a wonderful husband, two sons, and a home near her family of origin. Then tragedy struck the economy, and her little family was forced to move to another city to find work and housing.

The young mother watched her two boys grow up and marry two lovely young women in their new community. Then, without warning, tragedy and death struck the household as the wife and mother lost first her husband and then her two sons. When the grief-stricken, widowed mother-in-law chose to return to her birthplace, she cried out, "Don't call me Naomi . . . Call me Mara, because the Almighty has made my life very bitter. I went away full, but the Lord has brought me back empty" (Ruth 1:20–21).

Mara, the Hebrew word meaning "bitter," carries a harsh sting. Naomi simply wanted a normal life, but she lost everything. Her future looked bleak. She could not see God's grace or loving-kindness in her dire circumstances. In fact, she blamed

God for her bitter plight. How many of us have also come to that place of bitterness and blame when tragedy struck?

Bitterness is a root that can grow deep into our lives. In Hebrews 12:15, the writer states, "See to it that no one falls short of the grace of God and that no bitter root grows up to cause trouble and defile many." While most roots grow down, the root of bitterness grows up into the very places we least expect it to grow. It destroys our relationships and our future. Bitterness causes havoc and destroys everything around us.

Paul the apostle writes, "Get rid of all bitterness" (Ephesians 4:31). The idea of getting rid of something elicits the image of digging up weeds and throwing them away. Is the digging up process easy? No. But God provides grace for each of our losses. His grace is sufficient and can provide the contentment we need when we feel everything is gone.

Ask for God's grace. He promises a generous supply.

Father, forgive me for blaming you and others for my hurt, pain, and losses. Help me to experience your grace, not just my pain. Teach me to be content with what you have given me today. I give you thanks in Jesus' name. Amen.

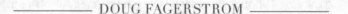

———————— DOUG FAGERSTROM ————————

Dealing with Unresolved Grief

Read: Job 29:1–6

Job cried out, longing for the time when his children were still alive and God still watched over him. In prior chapters, Job also longed for justice, for his day in court. In Job 29, he is still waiting. Those impacted by death due to violence may be able to relate to Job's powerful grief as a victim of violent crime.

When we lose loved ones due to homicide, not only is the death traumatizing but our grieving can also be interrupted while we are participating in or waiting on the criminal justice system. The investigations, the evidence gathering, the frequent media attention, the preliminary hearings, and the ensuing trials can all interfere with processing feelings of grief. As we face these necessary but draining details, we may choose to postpone our grief and leave it unresolved for a time.

Lew Cox's phone was ringing when he entered his office after a lengthy missionary trip to the Philippines. His son Darren's voice quivered on the other end as he delivered the life-changing news: "Dad, Carmon was murdered two days ago." Lew's lovely twenty-two-year-old daughter had been shot.

In a booklet coauthored with Bob Baugher titled *Coping with*

Traumatic Death: Homicide,[8] Lew describes the moments that followed.

> I had to do something, so I picked up a broom from my office and I started to sweep the carpet, saying to myself, "What am I going to do? What am I going to do?" As I dropped the broom and broke down sobbing, the surging emotions gripped me like a vise. Then, suddenly, all my emotions were attacked much like a shark in its feeding frenzy. I had no idea a human being could feel such deep grievous pain.

In the pages that follow, Lew, a police chaplain, weaves his story with sound advice for those dealing with traumatic death due to homicide. For Lew, enduring eighteen months of waiting for the case to proceed to trial was a roller-coaster ride. Lew survived by reminding himself, "One day at a time."

Eighteen years after Carmon's murder, Lew delivered an impact statement at a parole hearing for Carmon's slayer. When Lew started to talk, his jaw began to quiver, and moments later everything froze—his mouth, his brain, his body. He had no idea there was so much emotion still left unresolved.

In Job, we witness the intense grief of a father. Often neglected in an understanding of Job's lament is his wait for justice, his unresolved grief. And still, he chose to trust.

> *Dear Father, my grief is often overwhelming. In my waiting, help me to trust you. Amen.*

——————— DAVE BEACH ———————

46

Meditate on God's Word

Read: Psalm 1

My mom died when a drunk driver's car crashed into our van. My husband and six-year-old daughter were injured, and I wasn't expected to live. Because I was in the hospital, I missed Mom's funeral. After returning home, I sat and slept in a recliner in the living room and relied on others to help with simple tasks. My Bible and notebook were either on my lap or next to me during my weeks of recuperation. God spoke to me in many ways as I let his words sink into my heart and mind, and I delighted in that time spent with him.

After my body healed, reality set in. I was thirty-three years old, and both of my parents were gone. I felt like an orphan. As I read my Bible, God gave me the words I needed to hear and remember: "I will not leave you as orphans; I will come to you" (John 14:18).

Those who delight in and meditate on God's Word are "blessed" (see Psalm 1:1–2). God communicates with us through his Word. He knows what troubles us. He understands our needs. And Scripture comes alive as we ask him to speak to us. When we meditate on the verses he shows us, we receive comfort and peace in knowing how much he cares. Our focus turns to God rather than our circumstances.

Consider these suggestions as you read God's Word:

- Underline or highlight verses that are meaningful to you. God will draw you to those Scriptures when you need a reminder of his love or encouragement.
- Pray for God to reveal deeper meanings just for you and to fill your mind with his truths.
- On sheets of paper or in a notebook, write verses that speak comfort to you during times of sorrow or promises that you need to remember.
- Copy meaningful Scripture verses onto sticky notes and place them in prominent locations in your home, workplace, or car so that you can read them throughout the day.
- Pray the words back to God and thank him for how he's using them in your life.

The more you concentrate on God's Word, the more you will be blessed.

Lord, your words bring comfort, encouragement, and strength to me in my lowest times. Help me to savor the verses you give me and bring them to my mind throughout the day and night. Amen.

TWILA BELK

47

Do Not Let Your Heart Be Troubled

Read: Psalm 4 and John 14:1–9

D o not let your hearts be troubled," Jesus said to his disciples in John 14:1. But they were troubled. As the disciples shared dinner with Jesus, their hearts were burdened. During their last meal together, Jesus had predicted Judas's betrayal, warned Peter of his coming denial, and foretold his own impending death.

Yes, the disciples had a lot to be sorrowful about. Jesus had given them a glimpse of the future, and it overwhelmed them.

Grief is a paradox. On one hand, grief suspends us in time, bringing everything to an immediate standstill. On the other hand, grief has the capacity to launch us into a fabricated future of our own design. Constructing worst-case scenarios can propel us into situations God may never have intended for us. The challenge of the grief season, then, is to stay in the present without being overcome by the pain.

When Jesus said, "Do not let your hearts be troubled," he was saying that even in our darkest hour, during the most horrific pain we will ever know, even in that moment, we have a choice.

And then take a look at these words in James 1:4: "Let persever-ance finish its work so that you may be mature and complete." Is the Bible saying we have control over our own hearts when grief overwhelms us? We can choose to not be troubled. We can choose to allow perseverance to do its work even during the most soul-searing loss. We can cooperate with the pain.

How is that even possible?

To have a troubled heart is to believe we don't have the resources necessary to handle the pain. It isn't true, but that's what we believe because grief has invaded our hearts and cap-tured our perspective. The gulf between our sorrow and God's serenity feels too vast, too wide, and too difficult to traverse, so we remain troubled.

The antidote for a troubled heart is to stay in the present and believe. "Believe," Jesus said to his disciples. "You believe in God; believe also in me" (John 14:1). When we intentionally choose to believe in Jesus, we recognize that he does have the ability to provide what we need. Jesus promised to gift us with the Holy Spirit in John 14:16 and to give us his peace in John 14:27, so our move to belief is a tangible demonstration of our unity with him.

> *Lord, when I am tempted to lose that heart and doubt you are my resource, remind me that you are my bridge to healing. Help me remain confident of your presence in my pain as you provide peace for my present. Amen.*

DONNA TALLMAN

48

Grief Lasts Longer Than Expected

Read: Psalm 6

While I was reading a website offering medical advice, I noticed an article on grief. It said, "You should begin to feel better in six to eight weeks." That statement seemed like wishful thinking. We may want the effects of grief to be brief. We may hope to feel better after the typical three-day leave from work for a death in the family. Returning to work, we might long to compartmentalize the various parts of our self and take the grief out only when it is convenient—or not at all. That would be nice. Perhaps you have even done so. But chances are that this has not been your experience.

For most of us impacted by deep grief, grief lasts longer than expected and affects us in unexpected ways. In Psalm 6:3, the psalmist David leaves no uncertainty about grief's enduring symptoms as he laments, "How long, Lord, how long?" David also describes many symptoms, not only emotional but also physical and spiritual. He describes being faint, his bones in agony, his soul in deep anguish, and being worn out from groaning. Weeping all night long, he floods his bed with tears. His eyes grow weak with sorrow. The symptoms described are, in fact, remarkably consistent with our knowledge regarding the effects of grief.

Like David, we may feel the toll of grief in many ways: in our sleep, in our appetite, in our energy levels, and in our breathing. We may experience stress-related symptoms in heart palpitations, blood pressure, headaches, stomachaches, and other body pains. We may also find our immune system unable to fend off colds and flu and fight infections. Often other ailments and symptoms may seem unrelated to grief, but like a constellation, they emerge from or are intensified by grief.

Thinking back to my own experiences with grief, my worst times came three to five months after the loss. My sleep was disrupted; I lost weight; I had decreased interest in my usual hobbies, and I experienced a paroxysmal tachycardia—a false rhythm generated by the upper chamber of my heart. Fortunately, it is more of a nuisance than a danger.

Our experiences with grief may differ. Our symptoms will probably vary because of differing factors. But one thing will not vary: the unfailing love of our Lord, who invites us to share our grief and sorrow with him. We, too, are invited to cry out to him.

Dear Jesus, you are the Great Physician. Your touch heals and makes whole. My whole being feels my grief. Hear my cry for mercy and heal me. Amen.

DAVE BEACH

49

Never Alone

Read: Psalm 9:1–10

I was alone and frightened. I was lost and scared to death. At the age of nine, I found myself separated from my family in the underground tunnels of the Chicago subway system. This was my first time in this subterranean world. After passing several subway stops while seated among strangers, I began to cry.

I will never forget the lady in a ragged, gray wool coat who saw my tears, sat beside me, and kindly asked if I needed help. In my shaky voice, I eked out my dire circumstances. I can still hear her unforgettable words: "I will help you find your dad." At the next stop, she did just that. The mysterious lady in the tattered coat provided God-like comfort to a scared little boy. The nameless stranger became a living reminder that God will never forsake me. Psalm 9:10 was true.

The unforsaking presence of God in our worst times is described in 2 Corinthians 1:3–4: "The Father of compassion and the God of all comfort . . . comforts us in all our troubles, so that we can comfort those in any trouble." The word *comfort* is often used in conjunction with God's Spirit, as one who comes alongside us. Comfort is the lady in the wool coat. She just knew I was in trouble. She took the first step and came alongside me in my trouble. She became the comfort of a God who never forsakes us.

God is compassionate. He steps into our lives and he is there! We then have the capacity to offer comfort to others just like God has done for us.

I remember attending a visitation evening for a friend whose wife died. When I stood beside him by her casket, I never said a word. I hugged my friend, and together we embraced, arm in arm, remembering the joy of a life now gone. Later he told me how much comfort I had provided for him with no words said. I could not forsake my friend.

The parable of the good Samaritan (see Luke 10:25–37) illustrates how to not forsake others. The Samaritan compassionately saw the need of a stranger and took the first step. At the end of the story, Jesus says to all of us, "Go and do likewise" (verse 37).

You may one day meet a forsaken, hurting stranger—just as I was on that subway train. Compassionately offer comfort. Take the first step and remember, Jesus is our comfort.

Father, forgive me for passing by so many hurting people and doing nothing. Give me a heart of compassion. Give me the courage to take the first step and offer comfort as you have done for me. Amen.

DOUG FAGERSTROM

50

God Defends the Fatherless

Read: Psalm 10:12–18

I was thirty-eight when I lost my dad. "Old enough," I'd thought, to not need him so much anymore.

But I was desperately wrong. My grief stunned me with its intensity and left me not only missing my dad but feeling a gaping loss of fathering in my life. Who would cheer on my successes and pray for my challenges? Who would be there when my son made the junior varsity hockey team and when my daughter was having trouble with "mean girls" at school?

You have only one dad in this world, and when he dies, it's as if the earth cracks open. It feels as if your North Star has burned out, leaving you to grope aimlessly in a dark and moonless night.

When my dad died, too young and with too many years of parenting and grandparenting unlived, I had two choices: flounder without a father or embrace the fact that God is my Father in every single way.

When I began to look to God as my dad, I realized he had been my perfect hands-on dad all the time. I just hadn't seen his fathering in action the way I do now. God may not drive me up to the front door of church or of the mall on a snowy day so I don't have to walk in the cold, but he can help me find a parking spot and walk with me to the door. He is with us and for us 24/7, attending to even our practical needs.

Psalm 10:14 promises us that God is "the helper of the fatherless." He is "on call" night and day, with loving arms of comfort and protection. "Remain in my love," Jesus says in John 15:9. Stay in God's love; live there like a daughter lives under her father's roof, cherished and safe, the apple of his eye.

Who can we go to for wisdom and guidance? To God the Father, who gives generously; all we have to do is ask. Who is always there to cheer us on? Our Abba, Father (see Romans 8:15), who sings over his children with delight. If you've lost your father and lost your way—even a little bit—turn today to the Father who never takes his eyes off you. If your earthly dad wasn't perfect (and whose was?), God longs to heal your father wounds and establish the kind of parent-child relationship you've always dreamed of.

You'll always miss your dad, but know this: God your Father is waiting to enfold you with open arms. Get to know the Father to the fatherless better, starting today.

> *Lord, you are the father who longs to parent his children. Please help me to realize how deeply and perfectly you can fill the empty space left behind by my dad. Amen.*

LORILEE CRACKER

51

Grief Can't Be Rushed

Read: Psalm 13

Grief and sorrow wear us out; they exhaust us. We want so much to return to the way things were, our old normal. Or, accepting our loss, we may want desperately to find our new normal, to be done carrying this exhausting grief. We want to rush through the valley of sorrows and get to the other side. Our body, in response to the stress of acute grief, secretes hormones to bolster our immune system and to increase our ability to tolerate stress. Over time, however, even our bodies wear out from the stress of deep grief. Our whole being wants to be done with pain and sorrow, but grief cannot be rushed.

In Psalm 13, David wrestled day after day with thoughts and feelings, and he lamented, "How long?" This ancient lament so appropriately names our lament today. Like the question "Why?"—humankind's other primordial lament—this question, "How long?" echoes down through the ages in a chorus of groans.

What we hear in this psalm, at the very least, is a companion for the valley—someone to whom we can relate. We also hear permission for groaning. The psalms provide for us, as they provided for Jesus, a hymnal of the heart to teach us how to praise and how to lament, how to glorify and how to groan, how to bless and how to sing the blues. Not only are they the psalmists' gifts to the nation of Israel and the world, but they are also God's gift to us. God is saying to us through them, "I want you to talk to me about your feelings, and I want you to talk to me in these ways—ask me these questions, pour out these laments. I am your God and there are no others. Pray to me in these ways, and groan."

The apostle Paul understood this and wrote, "We know that the whole creation has been groaning as in the pains of childbirth right up to the present time. Not only so, but we ourselves, who have the first fruits of the Spirit, groan inwardly as we wait eagerly for our adoption to sonship, the redemption of our bodies" (Romans 8:22–23).

Even when we do not know what to say or what to pray, God groans for us. "We do not know what we ought to pray for, but the Spirit himself intercedes for us through wordless groans" (Romans 8:26).

Voicing this ancient lament in our grief, we join creation's chorus of groans waiting for our redemption.

> *Father God, you allowed all of creation to experience frustration in order to birth hope in us. I consent to your Spirit's work in me. Grant me patience as I long for our deliverance and the coming glory you call us to as your children. Amen.*

DAVE BEACH

52

Christ-Centered New Relationships

Read: Psalm 16

I woke up ashamed. In thirty-two years of marriage, I'd never dreamed about another man, and just five months after the death of my husband, I was hugging someone else in a dream. I'd loved David so much, how could I have thoughts of replacing him so soon, even in slumber? But moments later, I wondered if God might have sent my dream. After all, the Bible told me that he sometimes leads people through dreams. But over the following days, I prayerfully considered whether a new relationship at this point in my life would be God-centered, and I knew the answer was no. I was lonely, but I knew that basing a relationship on a random dream would be the worst thing I could do for my children or my own fragile emotions.

"That is why a man leaves his father and mother and is united to his wife, and they become one flesh," Genesis 2:24 says. No wonder the loss of a spouse is particularly painful. After the death of a spouse, we might feel as though we are left with a huge gaping wound. H. Norman Wright describes it as living "without." "We need to relearn who we will be 'without' the other and how we function. We need to relearn ourselves since when we lose someone we lose part of ourselves," he writes in *Reflections of a Grieving Spouse*.[9]

The loneliness of going from couple to self, from whole to part, makes a grieving spouse vulnerable. We need to take the time to relearn who we are without that other person. A surviving spouse should approach any new relationship with extreme caution. An active prayer life can help us be strong as we wait to see what God has in store for us.

Only one relationship can truly heal your broken heart. In Psalm 16, David confessed, "You are my Lord; apart from you I have no good thing" (verse 2) and "I keep my eyes always on the Lord. With him at my right hand, I will not be shaken" (verse 8). Use your loneliness to draw closer to God, for that is the most satisfying relationship of all. Immerse yourself in his Word. Join a Bible study or a Christian-based support group.

Have you figured out who you are "without"? If you are considering entering into any new relationship, ask yourself if it is what God would have for you or if your desire is me-centered, stemming from loneliness.

> *Lord, I am so lonely. You gifted me with a person who made me feel complete, and now I feel as though I am missing a part of myself. I ask for discernment regarding any future relationships. Amen.*

MARY POTTER KENYON

Discovering Strength
in Weakness

Read: Psalm 18:1–36

My husband's brother was killed in a snowmobile accident when our son, Jared, was eight years old. We were stunned and grieving, yet in the week between his uncle's death and the funeral, Jared was incredibly naughty. He seemed angry and confused, and he acted out in ways that seemed far beyond just grief.

Only God could have prompted my question: "Jared, do you know what a funeral is?" He looked so relieved when he said he didn't. I explained what a funeral was, what the funeral home would look like, who would be there, and what we would do after the service. We talked about the grave and the hearse, how we would stay in a hotel, how Jared could talk to his cousin, Blake, whose dad had just died. Jared visibly relaxed. His frown disappeared and his behavior improved.

While my young son couldn't express his confusion except through bad behavior, the apostle Paul certainly could express himself. He talked openly about his weaknesses because they brought him closer to Christ and brought the power of Christ into his life. Experts have long debated what Paul's "thorn in my flesh" that he mentions in 2 Corinthians 12:7 might have been. We'll never know, but perhaps that's the point. Whatever that weakness was, it brought the world's greatest missionary to his knees before the risen Christ.

Paul knew what it was to be weak; he knew about suffering and misery and hardship. Yet he understood that the bad stuff—whatever made him weak—actually strengthened his reliance on the Savior. Paul didn't diminish or ignore the bad; he simply turned to Christ for help and strength.

I know a young mother whose husband was diagnosed with cancer and given three months to live. She told me that she couldn't get through even a half hour at his bedside without reading Scripture. In the face of terrible tragedy, her source of strength was the very words of God.

My son turned to me in his confusion, and that woman turned to Scripture, just as Paul turned to Christ in his weakness and David turned to the Lord in his distress. Where are you turning in your time of mourning and difficulty? Are you turning to Christ, who can turn weakness into strength? Are you clinging to the Lord for your security? I pray that you are.

Father, take those things that I hold on to—fear, anger, control, confusion—and break me. Make me weak so I can become strong in you. Only in you will I flex the muscles of faith and love—and grow strong. Amen.

ANN BYLE

54

Time in God's Word

Read: Psalm 19

S andy was four months pregnant when an ultrasound revealed her unborn son didn't have a brain. "He will die shortly after birth," the doctor told her and her husband, Wayne.

Wayne and Sandy were devastated. Sandy said, "It was like the blackest black I can ever describe."

But even in the darkness, Sandy experienced the power of God's Word. A few days before the ultrasound, she had been reading her Bible. The words of Isaiah 26:3 resonated with her, so she marked and dated the verse, which says, "You will keep in perfect peace those whose minds are steadfast, because they trust in you."

The verse carried Sandy through the dark days after her son's diagnosis and through many sleepless nights during her pregnancy. After Ethan's delivery, Sandy looked up and saw Isaiah 26:3 printed on a poster in her hospital room. Once again, God's Word was a source of comfort and peace to Sandy and Wayne, an assurance of his active presence in their lives.

In *Spiritual Disciplines for the Christian Life*,[10] Don Whitney says, "A pertinent scriptural truth, brought to your awareness by the Holy Spirit at just the right moment, can be the weapon that makes the difference in a spiritual battle." And grief is a battle. A battle to trust the God who allowed a loved one to die. A battle to cling to hope when our hearts despair. A battle to believe what is unseen when we want concrete proof of God's presence.

Our greatest weapon in the battle with grief is God's Word. Psalm 19:7 says, "The law of the Lord is perfect, refreshing the soul. The statutes of the Lord are trustworthy, making wise the simple." This verse says God's Word has the ability to refresh our souls, to strengthen our faith, and to bring us wisdom when our judgment is clouded by loss.

But we reap these benefits only when we spend consistent time in Scripture. That's not easy under normal circumstances. When we're consumed by sorrow, it seems impossible. But the assurances gleaned from consistent time in God's Word can lighten our sorrow. So open your Bible each day. Read God's promises and allow them to lead you out of your present darkness into his everlasting light.

> *Dear Father, my heart wants to benefit from your word, but my spirit is weak. Grant me resolve to spend time in your word daily and to be comforted by it. Thank you for the gift of your word. Amen.*

JOLENE PHILO

55

Doubting Our Faith

Read: Psalm 22:1–8

Divine abandonment language confronts us in Psalm 22:1–8: "My God, my God, why have you forsaken me? Why are you so far from saving me, so far from my cries of anguish?" (verse 1). The psalmist remembers the faith of his ancestors: "In you our ancestors put their trust; they trusted and you delivered them. To you they cried out and were saved; in you they trusted and were not put to shame" (verses 4–5).

This is the pattern of deliverance: distress, lament, and then deliverance/salvation. The great faith of the psalmist's ancestors resulted in deliverance, but the unanswered cries of his faith gave rise to doubt. Sometimes, along with grief, we struggle with doubt.

I remember my own struggle with doubt. For over two months, my wife had been in a critical care unit in the Mayo Clinic complex in Rochester, Minnesota. Each morning and through the night, I prayed for Sue's healing. Reading through the psalms, I found Psalm 41 and prayed it over her:

> Blessed is Sue, who has regard for the weak;
>> the Lord delivers her in times of trouble.

The Lord protects Sue and preserves her—
>   she is counted among the blessed in the land—
>   he does not give her over to the desire of her foes.

The Lord sustains Sue on her sickbed
>   and restores her from her bed of illness (verses 1–3).

When she died, the words of Psalm 22:1–8 became my prayer, and I doubted my faith. It must have been the wrong kind, or maybe it was not enough. Doubting my faith was easier than admitting I felt abandoned. Admitting I felt abandoned seemed too risky.

Impugning my faith came easy. I could think of all the reasons it would be insufficient, inadequate, or ineffective. What, however, would I do with the faith of others who prayed? Before we left for Mayo Clinic, our church circulated a prayer card with a time slot for every half hour, around the clock, of every day. During Sue's stay at Mayo, different people had pledged to pray for each and every slot. Could I impugn their faith?

Soon Jesus' words from the cross gave me refuge. Quoting Psalm 22:1, he cried, "My God, my God, why have you forsaken me?" (Mark 15:34). What I needed was the courage to speak them.

> *Father, help me in my faith to voice this risky lament speech— the language of suffering Jesus voiced from the cross. Give me the courage of Jesus to convey the depths of my heart so his image may be formed there—especially there. Amen.*

—————— DAVE BEACH ——————

56

Shock and Numbness

Read: Psalm 23

The sound of my friend Stephanie's voice was serious. She went on to deliver the news that my best friend of thirty-five years had been in a terrible car accident. My mind raced, and I tried to brace myself for what she was about say.

"I'm sorry to tell you this, Lori."

Time stood still and numbness spread from my chest to my stomach and down my arms.

"No, no, no! Don't say it!" I tried to push away what I already knew in my heart.

"She didn't make it."

"Can't they do something for her?" I yelled.

"She died two days ago. I'm so sorry."

I fell to my knees. The words took my breath away as I entered the lowest point of my life. My best friend was gone. A repeat drunk driver had killed her. I couldn't take in the truth. It didn't seem real. I was in shock.

It's been five and a half years since Shannon died, and throughout the process of my grief, I've come to appreciate the gift of shock. Shock and numbness form God's pause button.

During this time, he wraps his arms around us and whispers, "Hold on. I'm here."

In John 16, when Jesus told his disciples he was going to leave them, surely they were upset. Their lives revolved around him, so they must have felt incredibly powerless and shocked about the news that he was going to leave them. In the midst of their confusion, Jesus said to them, "You will weep and mourn while the world rejoices. You will grieve, but your grief will turn to joy" (verse 20). Jesus cast a vision beyond their impending suffering; he gave them the promise of eternal hope beyond their pain. He gives that same hope to us.

God will walk you through each step of grief until you're with him for eternity. He's with you in the midst of your most excruciating pain. As David, the shepherd and psalmist, declared, "The Lord is my shepherd, I lack nothing . . . Even though I walk through the darkest valley, I will fear no evil, for you are with me; your rod and your staff, they comfort me" (Psalm 23:1, 4).

Take one day at a time, and remember you don't have to power through your sadness alone. God gives supernatural comfort. He gently says to you, "Hold on. I'm here."

Jesus, you see my pain and my desperate heart. Thank you for your promise to someday turn my grief to joy. Help me to feel your comforting presence with me when I can't feel that reality through my grief. Amen.

LORI LARA

57

Touch Someone's Life
in Your Grief

Read: Psalm 25:1–8

W hat do you do to make yourself feel better when things get really bad?" The question from the group facilitator hung in the air.

I waited quietly. I was new to the grief support group and the most recently widowed. Surely someone else in the room could offer some sage advice. No one spoke. I hesitated briefly before sharing one of the ways I'd found comfort and strength.

"For weeks I dreaded Tuesdays. The second day of the week became a reminder of my loss. I counted the weeks, one after another, until one morning I couldn't bear to face another Tuesday. I had to change the meaning of the day. So I began my odyssey of reaching out to others that morning, then every week through a card or a letter. Soon I began looking forward to Tuesday with anticipation. Who would I reach out to that day? Now every Tuesday my mailbox is full of outgoing mail."

"Forget the former things; do not dwell on the past," Isaiah 43:18 says. I will never really forget that Tuesday is the day of the week my husband died, but I had a choice: I could make something positive out of the day instead of dwelling on his death.

Second Corinthians 1:3–4 tells us, "Praise be to the God and Father of our Lord Jesus Christ, the Father of compassion and the God of all comfort, who comforts us in all our troubles, so that we can comfort those in any trouble with the comfort we ourselves receive from God."

Our suffering can be a direct link to Jesus Christ. If we allow it, God can use our time of grieving to help us to grow in compassion so we can then minister to others. God's amazing comfort spills over into our lives, giving us increased empathy and compassion. Dr. Larry Crabb agrees: "Sometimes the best remedy for grief is finding some way to touch someone else's life."[11]

Are you open to God's path in your own grief experience? Can you use your suffering as a means of spiritual growth? Are you at a point in your grieving where you might feel comfortable reaching out to others? What can you do for someone today?

Dear Lord, thank you for the people you have brought into my life to comfort me. Help me to discover ways to use my grief to become a more compassionate person and do your work. Teach me your truths that can give meaning to my suffering. Amen.

——————— MARY POTTER KENYON ———————

58

We Shall Know Fully

Read: Psalm 26

O nce you become aware that the main business you are here for is to know God, most of life's problems fall into place of their own accord." So says J. I. Packer, the author of *Knowing God*.[12] But can that statement apply to grieving people? Can knowing God really help someone deal with grief and loss? Or can he use grief and loss to help us to know him more fully?

David and Nancy Guthrie asked those questions when their newborn daughter, Hope, and later, their in-utero son, Gabriel, were diagnosed with a rare metabolic disorder. Both babies died before they were six months old. Nancy says that through the difficult months of caring for terminally ill children, she came to believe what she knew about God. "It is one thing to believe that God is faithful and will supply all your needs—even in the darkest times. It is another thing to experience it," she says in *Holding On to Hope: A Pathway Through Suffering to the Heart of God*.[13]

Trying to know God when our hearts ache may seem overwhelming. But Nancy explains how she came to know him best through her pain. "We recognize that we are powerless and that he is powerful. We pray and we see him more clearly because we are desperately looking for him . . . This is always God's purpose: to use whatever means he sees fit to bring us to a closer relationship with him, to create in us a faith that will give us the strength to keep holding onto hope . . . genuine biblical hope that one day what is unseen will be seen."

Paul referred to this hope in 2 Corinthians 4:17–18. "For our light and momentary troubles are achieving for us an eternal glory that far outweighs them all. So we fix our eyes not on what is seen, but on what is unseen, since what is seen is temporary, but what is unseen is eternal."

What is our unseen hope? To realize that through knowing God, the most heart-wrenching problems of life can fall into place. To one day join our children, and all the loved ones gone before us who trusted Jesus as Savior, in heaven. To one day see God face-to-face. And to spend eternity praising the God who used our pain and suffering to draw us to the one in whom we are fully known.

This is our hope. Alleluia!

> *Lord God, I want to know you more. I want to believe in you. So, please use my loss to help me see you more clearly. Grow my faith so I come to believe you are who you say you are. Amen.*

JOLENE PHILO

59

Be Strong and Take Heart

Read: Psalm 31

By ministering to women who've endured miscarriage, stillbirth or infant loss, and having experienced loss myself, I am all too familiar with these situations. One common thread among these stories is that parents often feel unsupported. The experience of miscarriage tends to be a disenfranchised grief in our society. People tend to convey a "try again" mentality to those who have lost a child. Equally hurtful are attempts to offer support by voicing insensitive comments or unwelcome Christian clichés. Perhaps you have been on the receiving end of such support.

Psalm 31 provides wonderful encouragement and points us to our reliable source of hope and healing. Throughout the psalm, the character of God starkly contrasts with the people who surrounded David, the author of the psalm. In verse 7, David expresses his knowledge of God's love for him by saying, "I will be glad and rejoice in your love, for you saw my affliction and knew the anguish of my soul." If you are feeling misunderstood and unsupported by those in your world, may the truth of God's love and understanding bring you comfort.

God possesses an intimate knowledge of you (see Psalm 139), and he knows your heart (see Luke 16:15). He knows your every need. Jesus himself declared, "Your Father knows what you need before you ask him" (Matthew 6:8). Rest in these truths.

On a practical level, it's important that we are equipped to respond to others with grace. As you cope with hurtful comments or clichés, consider the following questions to help you reframe and cope with the comment in a positive way.

- Who is the person who made the comment?
- What is my relationship with this person?
- What do I value in my relationship with this person?
- What was the source of the comment, and how did I perceive it?
- What do I believe are the true motives or intentions of this person?

You will likely find that the person's insensitive comment or their perceived lack of support is actually an attempt to protect you or to convey care and concern. Receive comments with grace, and remember the true source of your strength: your God who knows you. He is the only one who can fully satisfy your expectations and needs. He is the giver of all hope.

Lord, help me to rely on you during this time of grief. I trust you to be my refuge and my strength. Amen.

TESKE DRAKE

60

Grief Is Not Forever

Read: Psalm 30

As I carried a basket of laundry down the basement steps one morning approximately four months after my husband's death, it suddenly occurred to me that I hadn't cried once in the previous twenty-four hours—not even a stifled sob in the darkness of the night. The basket slid from my hands, splaying dirty laundry all over the steps. I sat down and started sobbing uncontrollably—crying about not crying because I never wanted to forget David.

After the death of her husband, author Madeleine L'Engle wrote in *Two-Part Invention: The Story of a Marriage*, "But grief still has to be worked through. It is like walking through water. Sometimes there are little waves lapping about my feet. Sometimes there is an enormous breaker that knocks me down. Sometimes there is a sudden and fierce squall."[14]

It is that sudden and fierce squall that knocks us flat, leaves us gasping for breath and choking down sobs. Will we always feel like our heart has been torn in two? Or if the pain is abating, does it mean we are forgetting our loved one?

"Your sun will never set again, and your moon will wane no

more; the Lord will be your everlasting light, and your days of sorrow will end," the prophet Isaiah said (Isaiah 60:20).

God promises our sorrow will end. It is somehow easier to endure distress if we know that an end is in sight and that this grief-filled time is but a "season" in our life. Ecclesiastes 3:1–4 says, "There is a time for everything, and a season for every activity under the heavens: a time to be born and a time to die, a time to plant and a time to uproot, a time to kill and a time to heal, a time to tear down and a time to build, a time to weep and a time to laugh, a time to mourn and a time to dance."

Are you at that point yet? Are you ready to dance? One day you will wake up and realize you have not wept or uttered the name of your deceased loved one for twenty-four hours. Another day you might catch yourself laughing with abandon. This is good; it means the dark burden of grief is lifting. In response to God's deliverance in a time of distress, David proclaimed to the Lord, "You turned my wailing into dancing; you removed my sackcloth and clothed me with joy" (Psalm 30:11).

Have you felt guilty for laughing or smiling? Remember that the person you lost would want to see you happy. Be grateful to God for those moments of pleasure you are able to experience in spite of your pain.

> *Dear Lord, some days my sorrow feels unending. I am constantly reminded of my loss. Hear my cries and help me find joy again. Amen.*

——————— MARY POTTER KENYON ———————

Notes

1. James W. Pennebaker, *Opening Up* (New York: Guilford, 1990), 34.
2. Charles Spurgeon, *God Promises You* (New Kensington, PA: Whitaker House, 1995), 167–68.
3. "News You Can Use," *U.S. News and World Report*, October 18, 1991, 5.
4. Jack Jacobs, interview by Chris Jansing, *NBC Nightly News*, 15 June 2011.
5. Nancy Leigh DeMoss with Lawrence Kimbrough, *Choosing Gratitude: Your Journey to Joy* (Chicago: Moody, 2009), 17.
6. Oswald Chambers, "His Temptation and Ours," September 18, 2012, *My Utmost for His Highest*, http://utmost.org/classic/his-temptation-and-ours-classic/.
7. Jim Cymbala. *Fresh Wind, Fresh Fire* (Grand Rapids: Zondervan, 1997), 78.
8. Bob Baugher and Lew Cox, *Coping with Traumatic Death: Homicide* (self-published, 2011), 3.
9. H. Norman Wright, *Reflections of a Grieving Spouse* (Eugene, OR: Harvest House, 2009), 43.
10. Donald S. Whitney, *Spiritual Disciplines for the Christian Life* (Colorado Springs: NavPress, 1991), 42.

11. Larry Crabb, "7 Steps to Healthy Grieving," Evangelical Presbyterian Church of Annapolis newsletter, June/July/ August 2009, 7.
12. J. I. Packer, *Knowing God* (Downers Grove, IL: InterVarsity Press, 1973), 34.
13. Nancy Guthrie, *Holding On to Hope* (Carol Stream, IL: Tyndale, 2006), 86.
14. Madeleine L'Engle, *Two-Part Invention: The Story of a Marriage* (San Francisco: Harper San Francisco, 1988), 229.

About Contributors

CYNTHIA BEACH, longtime professor of creative writing at Cornerstone University, is also an author and serves as a writing and creativity coach through Soul Seasons (SoulSeasons.org). She holds an MFA in fiction and is the author of *The Surface of Water*.

DAVE BEACH lives with his wife, Cynthia, in rural Michigan. Dave learned of grief and loss through the deaths of his brother, Dick, in 1982, and his first wife, Sue, in 1991, after her six-year battle with lymphoma. Dave has been a director of counseling at Soul Seasons and a professor of social sciences at Cornerstone University. He is currently a hospice and bereavement volunteer and an ordained chaplain for First Responder Chaplains / International Association of Chaplains.

SHELLY BEACH is an award-winning author of more than a dozen books and specialty Bibles. She lives in Cedar Falls, Iowa, and is cofounder of the Cedar Falls Christian Writer's Workshop. She speaks nationally on a variety of issues and presents seminars for Daughters of Destiny national women's prison ministry.

TWILA BELK, aka the Gotta Tell Somebody Gal, enjoys speaking, writing, teaching at conferences and bragging on God. Twila's books include *Raindrops from Heaven, The Power to Be,* and four titles coauthored with veteran author Cecil Murphey.

DANIEL BERNSTROM spent his childhood writing children's books, short stories, and plays, but it wasn't until college that he realized writing would be his life's work. He holds an MFA in creative writing from Hamline University and is the critically acclaimed author of numerous books for children.

DAVE BRANON has been a contributing writer for Our Daily Bread for over three decades. He is the author of numerous books on sports, Christian living, the Bible, and grief.

TIMOTHY BURNS is a writer, speaker, and mentor to writers. He provides social media marketing services for an international client base and often writes about the unalterable connection between personal freedom, national liberty and intentional reliance on the living God.

ANN BYLE is a freelance writer for publications including *Today's Christian Woman* and *Publishers Weekly.* She is the author or coauthor of several books, including *Christian Publishing 101, The Joy of Working at Home,* and *Chicken Scratch: Lessons on Living Creatively from a Flock of Hens.*

LORILEE CRAKER is the author or coauthor of more than

a dozen books, including the Audie Award–nominee *Money Secrets of the Amish* and the ECPA best seller *My Journey to Heaven* with Marv Besteman. The experience of writing about heaven in depth was comforting and deeply inspiring and connected her to heaven in a way she had never been before.

DAWN SCOTT DAMON is a conference speaker and author who shares from her past struggles with openness and transparency. She is CEO and Founder of A Brave New Dawn and the BraveHearted Woman at A Brave New Dawn Enterprise. Dawn is the author of several books on trauma and overcoming.

TESKE DRAKE is a "mommy with hope" to three babies in heaven and a mother to two on earth. Teske has served as cofounder and president of Mommies with Hope, a biblically based ministry for women who have experienced the loss of a child through miscarriage, stillbirth, or infant loss. She earned her PhD in human development and family studies from Iowa State University. Her first book was *Hope for Today, Promises for Tomorrow: Finding Light Beyond the Shadow of Miscarriage or Infant Loss.*

SANDI ELZINGA is an award-winning author, book reviewer, and former newsletter editor. Her articles on grief and loss have been published in *The Christian Journal* and *In Touch* magazine. She is the author of *GriefWalk: Hope Through the Dark Places*, a blog for those who have lost a loved one, which includes a discussion page (*GriefTalk*), where those in grief offer comfort to one another. Sandi began and led a widow's support group.

DOUG FAGERSTROM and his wife, Donna, served the gospel of Jesus Christ in four churches over their first three decades of pastoral ministry. Doug then served in leadership positions at Converge Worldwide, Grand Rapids Theological Seminary before his retirement. Doug has written more than a dozen books published by Kregel, Baker, and Zondervan.

SUE FOSTER is a licensed marriage and family therapist specializing in grief counseling, especially with those who are grieving the loss of a loved one to suicide. Sue lost her daughter Shannon to suicide in 1991. Her resource book for survivors of suicide, *Finding Your Way After the Suicide of Someone You Love*, was coauthored with David Biebel. Sue has worked with survivors, trained therapists, spoken to students and at conferences, workshops and retreats, worked with various suicide organizations and facilitated faith-based support groups for survivors.

ALISON HODGSON is a gifted communicator who writes and speaks about all the gory details of following Jesus. Her writing has been published by Baker Publishing Group, Houzz.com, the Christianity Today blog for women her.meneutics, Religion News Service and praiseandcoffee.com.

When MARIA KECKLER was twelve her father underwent brain surgery and one week later lost the use of half of his body and most of his cognitive and speaking abilities. He died one year later at age thirty-nine. Maria serves as International Affairs Strategy and Communications Director at San Diego

State University. She has been published in Christian and secular markets, academic journals, online and trade publications, and books on Christian living as a ghostwriter and collaborator.

MARY POTTER KENYON has written over three hundred articles and essays published in magazines, newspapers, and anthologies, including five *Chicken Soup* books. She has also published books on cancer and grief, including *Refined by Fire: A Journey of Grief and Grace* with Cecil Murphey. Mary credits her mother's death in 2010 on Mary's fifty-first birthday for the gift of newfound faith and a personal relationship with Jesus Christ that brought her strength and comfort when her husband died unexpectedly just sixteen months later.

LORI LARA is a professional photographer, author, blogger and trauma survivor. She's passionate about helping others through hard times as she shares her continued story of spiritual healing from major depression, addiction, and PTSD. Her world was turned upside down again in 2012 when her mom was diagnosed with brain cancer.

JOLENE PHILO grew up with a father disabled by multiple sclerosis and is parent to a son with special medical needs. Though her father died in 1997 and her son is an independent adult, she still sometimes grieves for what her family lost. She is the author of several books on caregiving and special needs, and she speaks around the country about the grief and guilt struggles experienced by parents of children with special needs.

BETH ROBINSON, EdD, is an author, licensed professional counselor, and longtime professor of counseling at Lubbock Christian University. She specializes in counseling issues related to foster care, adoption, sexual abuse, and traumatized children.

NATASHA SISTRUNK ROBINSON is a graduate of the US Naval Academy (BS), Gordon-Conwell Theological Seminary (MA), and North Park Theological Seminary (DMin). She is president of T3 Leadership Solutions and founder of Leadership LINKS. Natasha writes and speaks worldwide on the topics of leadership, discipleship, mentoring, compassion, and justice.

DORIS SANFORD experienced the death of her husband when he fell in a mountain climbing accident. She was thirty-three years old and the mother of a newborn and a three-year-old. Since that time she has led support groups for grieving children, served as a church consultant for widows' issues, was on staff at a hospice, taught college courses on grief, and wrote a book for grieving children and another book for new widows. She is a frequent speaker about issues facing those who grieve.

SANDRA SCOTT, a licensed professional counselor, was in private practice for over thirty years before her retirement. She specialized in individual and family relationship issues. She has conducted numerous seminars on abuse and PTSD, primarily directed at educating church leaders and congregations to recognize and respond appropriately to all aspects of this major problem.

STEVE SILER is the founder and director of Music for the Soul, a multi-award-winning Christian music ministry creating unique song, testimony, and video recordings bringing hope and healing to people dealing with issues of deep pain. *More Beautiful* (breast cancer) and *Chaos of the Heart* (suicide grief) are just a few of the projects Steve has produced for Music for the Soul. Siler has written nine No. 1 contemporary Christian music songs, working with artists such as Point of Grace, Avalon, Anointed, Be Be Winans, and Larnelle Harris, among others.

DONNA TALLMAN has served as a screenwriter, conference speaker, mentor, curriculum developer, women's ministry coordinator, and teacher for all ages. She lives and writes in the greater Colorado Springs area.

PRAYER NOTES

....

....

....

....

....

....

....

....

....

....

PRAYER NOTES

....

....

....

....

....

....

....

....

....

....

....

PRAYER NOTES

....

....

....

....

....

....

....

....

....

....

....